FROM MANY CULTURES,
One HISTORY

The History of the
AMERICAN INDIANS
and the
RESERVATION

Judith Edwards

Enslow Publishers, Inc.
40 Industrial Road
Box 398
Berkeley Heights, NJ 07922
USA

http://www.enslow.com

Library of Congress Cataloging-in-Publication Data

Edwards, Judith, 1940–
    The history of the American Indians and the reservation / Judith Edwards.
        p. cm. — (From many cultures, one history)
      Summary: "Explores the difficult changes American Indians were forced to
make, including moving off their land, adapting to life on reservations, and how
those reservations have changed since their creation"—Provided by publisher.
    Includes bibliographical references and index.
    ISBN-13: 978-0-7660-2798-5
    ISBN-10: 0-7660-2798-8
    1. Indians of North America—Relocation—Juvenile literature. 2. Indian
reservations—Juvenile literature. 3. Indians of North America—Government
relations—Juvenile literature. 4. United States—Ethnic relations—Juvenile
literature. 5. United States—Race relations—Juvenile literature. I. Title.
  E98.R4E39 2008
  323.1197—dc22

                    2007028275

Printed in the United States of America

10 9 8 7 6 5 4 3 2 1

Illustration Credits: Associated Press, pp. 96, 101, 108, 112, 117; Cumberland County
Historical Society, p. 65; Getty Images, p. 55; The Granger Collection, pp. 13, 19, 21, 22,
50, 62, 76, 114, 115 (right); © Hammond World Atlas Corporation, NJ, Lic. No. 12569,
p. 6; Library of Congress, pp. 4, 44, 68, 73, 84, 116; National Archives an Records
Administration, pp. 46, 80, 89; The Newark Museum/Art Resource, NY, p. 9; North Wind
Picture Archives, p. 29; Paul Chesley/Getty Images, p. 104; Smithsonian American Art
Museum, Washington, D.C./Art Resource, NY, p. 35; Woolaroc Museum, Bartlesville,
Oklahoma, pp. 27, 115 (left).

Flag Illustration Used in Book Design: © 2007 Jupiter Images Corporation.

Cover Illustration: The Associated Press.

Contents

Sitting Bull felt that American Indians should fight against reservations because those who lived on the land got little support from the government.

CHAPTER One

Battling for Freedom

"Then another great cry went up out in the dust: 'Crazy Horse is coming!' Off toward the west and north, they were yelling 'Hoka Hey' like a big wind roaring, and making the tremolo; and you could hear eagle bone whistles screaming."[1]

Black Elk (Oglala Sioux), 1876

Two Moons was the leader of a Cheyenne Indian band. Like other Sioux and Cheyenne leaders, he opposed the United States's 1875 order that all Sioux live only on reservations. But buffalo and other game were scarce and his people were hungry. So Two Moons had decided that he would bring his band to a reservation in southeastern Montana. The Cheyenne had formed a village near the camp of

The map above shows where different American Indian nations lived before the arrival of European settlers.

Crazy Horse, an Ogala Sioux leader who resented being told to move onto a reservation. Crazy Horse was angry about broken treaties that had promised American Indians access to hunting lands in the Black Hills region of South Dakota and the Powder River and Big Horn countryside in Montana and

Wyoming. Meanwhile, white settlers and miners were taking over these lands.

One dawn, in March 1876, while the Cheyenne families led by Two Moons were asleep, six companies of U.S. Cavalry descended on the sleeping village. Quickly rising and summoning his warriors, Two Moons gathered the women and children and sent them to Crazy Horse's camp. Children were crying, their mothers were crying and comforting and hurrying, and the warriors were grabbing weapons.

Two Moons rallied his warriors and with great bravery counterattacked the cavalry. The Indians fought so fiercely that the soldiers turned their horses and galloped from the village, setting fire to tipis as they left. This attack, and the destruction of his village, angered Two Moons so much that his people camped with Crazy Horse and gave up the idea of entering a reservation.

The demand to submit to the reservation led Sitting Bull, a Hunkpapa Lakota leader whose opinion mattered to the Sioux, to remark with scorn that those who did not rebel against the reservation order and the rations it promised were "slaves to a piece of fat bacon, some hardtack [a stiff biscuit] and a little sugar and coffee."[2]

Before the Reservations

One estimate of the American Indian population in North and South America in 1491, the year before the arrival of the explorer Christopher Columbus, is truly astounding. Could there have been more than ninety million people living on these continents then?[1] This figure, calculated by anthropologist Henry A. Dobyns, has been disputed. However, it is based on scientific studies that are increasingly respected. This could mean that in 1491 there were more people living in the Americas than in Europe. (According to a 1999 estimate from the United Nations, there were about 500 million people living on earth at the beginning of the sixteenth century. The most densely populated area was Central America.)[2]

Columbus named these people "Indians" because he was trying to sail around the world to China and

In the painting Landing of Columbus, *by Albert Bierstadt in 1893, Caribbean Indians observe the arrival of the explorer.*

he thought he had landed in the East Indies when he arrived at islands in the Caribbean Sea, south of the United States. "Most Indians view the arrival of Columbus as the beginning of a four hundred year cycle of disease, exploitation, enslavement and genocide that devastated them as a race of people," says George Russell, an historian who is a Saginaw Chippewa Indian.[3] By 1900, American Indians numbered just 237,000, according to the official U.S. Census Bureau count.[4] "If Dobyns was right," says author Charles C. Mann, "disease claimed the lives of eighty to one hundred million Indians by the first third of the seventeenth century."[5] This would mean that 95 percent of the people living in America died in about 130 years of contact with Europeans.

American Indian Beginnings

Where did the Indians of America come from? And when did they arrive? Ideas vary, but one of the stronger theories is that there was one single migration, probably from the land now called Siberia in Russia, across either a land bridge or ice forming in the Bering Strait. The theoretical land bridge was part of a larger piece of land called Beringia. This single migration is thought to have taken place anywhere from thirty-three thousand to forty-three thousand years ago.[6] Another estimate puts this migration at as little as twenty thousand years ago.[7] Proponents of both estimates agree that the original migrants split off into two or three groups. This migration led to the populating of North, Central, and South America.

European Settlement

In some cases, American Indians greeted the European settlers, first at Jamestown in 1607 and in Plymouth in 1620, with generosity. They agreed to the settlers' occupying specific pieces of land. The Pilgrim colony at Plymouth, Massachusetts, learned how to survive in this new world because of the skills their

American Indian neighbors shared with them. In both colonies, when more people arrived who needed more land, it was just taken. Then conflict arose.

"From then on the Indian was in almost constant retreat before the stream of pioneers heading westward, where demand for land never ceased," says historian Ralph Andrist.[8]

However, long before the colonies at Jamestown and Plymouth were even thought of, European expeditions had changed the lives of the American Indians. There were about five hundred Indian groups in what is now the United States, all speaking different languages, according to author Russell Thornton.[9]

Popular stories and films show all American Indians living on the plains, riding horses, and living in tipis. They wear war paint and feathers. American Indians at the first Thanksgiving are shown sharing harvest food with the Pilgrims. The reality of American Indians is a much more diverse and complex picture.

In the southeastern part of North America, the American Indian grouping is called the Mississippian Culture, or the Mississippi Mound Civilization. This was not the nomadic culture of the Great Plains, but a people who were well-organized in seasonal farming communities. Contact in 1539 with an early Spanish explorer, Hernando De Soto, left this culture devastated from battle and disease.

By the mid-seventeenth century, when the English and French reached inland southeastern North America, the remaining Mississippian people had scattered. The culture evolved into different American Indian groups. The remaining bands of Mississippian Indians, disorganized and completely without their old stable social, religious, and family structure, became the Creek, Muskogee, Choctaw, Chickasaw, and Cherokee nations.

In the Northeast, the Algonquian-speaking peoples lived in present-day New York and Ohio. The Iroquoians lived on lands that included the interior waterways, especially around the Great Lakes. Six Iroquoian tribes—the Mohawk, Onondaga, Seneca, Oneida, Cayuga, and later, the Tuscarora—formed a group called the League of the Longhouse.

Again, an expedition of Europeans began to change the destiny of this powerful nation. Around 1550, during Jacques Cartier's exploration of the St. Lawrence River in what is now Quebec, Canada, European trade goods were introduced to the Iroquois. Iron tools, which reduced the amount of time needed to cut or scrape animal parts and hides, became particularly prized possessions. So did such items as beads, cloth, and mirrors, because they became status symbols. By the time the Dutch arrived in 1614 to build Fort Nassau near Albany, New York, the League's access and dependence on European goods was a fact of life. This affected not

An Algonquian village of 1590 North Carolina is depicted in this color engraving by Theodor de Bry after an illustration by John White. Cornfields can be seen at the right, and American Indians prepare food in the center of the picture.

only the Iroquois, but the powerful Huron who lived in the territory north and west of the Iroquois and Algonquian territories. The Huron maintained a powerful and complex trade network. Their nation was weakened by European disease, leaving them vulnerable to attack and social problems.

This unraveling of the American Indian world was going on simultaneously through all the land that would become the original thirteen colonies. The generosity with which the Wampanoag had greeted the new colonists at Plymouth was not returned. By 1633, the expanding Pilgrim colony had used all available land and found excuses to invade lands belonging to the surviving bands of Wampanoag.

A Life of Balance

All the Algonquian speakers, whether hunters or farmers, knew that corn had a 160-day growing season. In the fall, when the corn ripened, American Indian villages disbanded. Indians traveled with the seasons and the availability of game. They had no concept of individual land ownership. To them, land and sea and water were similar elements, and how can a person own any of those?

The Indians combined farming, gathering, hunting, and fishing. The colonists, who lived in permanent houses much more cramped and unhealthy than the Indian dwellings, had no understanding

"Stained With Blood"

From the account of a Chitmacha Indian survivor of the slave raids along the Mississippi River, 1718:

> The sun was red, the roads filled with brambles and thorns, the clouds were black, the water was troubled and stained with blood, our women wept unceasingly, our children cried with fright, the game fled far from us, our houses were abandoned, and our fields uncultivated, we all have empty bellies and our bones are visible.[10]

of the Indian "way of the land." They saw only that for part of a year land was unused, which made them think they had the right to take it over.

Deadly Disease

Diseases such as smallpox, cholera, and the flu killed more of the American Indian population over the years than armed conflict. Indians had no immunity to the diseases that were brought over by Europeans. Many American Indians were wiped out by disease—particularly smallpox. Struggling survivors were sometimes sold into slavery to work on plantations. These raids disrupted the agricultural cycle. People were afraid to go out hunting because of the raiders.

Villages full of people who were hungry and afraid were susceptible to diseases to which most white men had built up immunity for over many centuries. It became a vicious circle that led to devastation and death for American Indians.

CHAPTER Three

The Decline of Independence

By 1671, there were already fifty thousand Europeans living in the colonies in what would become the United States.[1] Though earlier settlers traded with and learned from the American Indians, the hunger for land changed that relationship. Americans labeled the Indians as uncivilized, even savage. They took over lands used by the Indians. Bounties (rewards of money) were sometimes placed on the scalps of Indian men, women, and children.

The Mighty Iroquois

The area near the eastern part of the border of what became Canada and the United States was the territory of the Iroquois. They were powerful allies of the British. The French were aligned with the Algonquin and had set up a string of trading posts for receiving valuable beaver pelts and dispensing

Rewarding Death

"In 1755 the British Crown offered 40 pounds for Indian male scalps and 20 pounds for women and children," says historian Richard White of a proclamation that was issued by the Governor of New England and posted throughout the countryside. In addition to the bounty on scalps, fifty pounds was offered for male prisoners over the age of twelve and twenty-five pounds for male and female prisoners under the age of twelve.[2]

European goods to the Indians. This was to lead to terrible consequences for the Indians, because they became more dependent on European goods, especially tools. Manufactured items always exceeded the value of what Indians could trade, so the balance of trade was unequal. American Indian lands were overhunted, depleting the game that supplied food and clothing. This led to the need to trap in areas used by other Indians, which led to warfare. Indians were coerced into selling land through treaties, which were hard for them to understand.

However, the French and the Iroquois coexisted as two sovereign nations—for a time that is. But from 1754 to 1763, the Iroquois joined the British in fighting the French and their Indian allies. This became known as the French and Indian War. Historian Richard White writes: "In hindsight the possibilities for Indian independence within the mixed political world of the mid-eighteenth century began to change in 1763 when England defeated France in the [French and Indian War.]"[3]

"The world of mutual dependence and accommodation, in which the Indians and the whites could find a place for one another, was disappearing," according to historian Landon Jones.[4]

Poor Treatment

Lord Jeffrey Amherst, the British army commander in North America, believed that after the war the American Indians were subjects of the British Crown. They had no choice but to do what Britain dictated.[5] The Delaware, Shawnee, and Ottawa nations, who had already been driven from their homelands in the East, rebelled against the British repression and against rival American Indians.

Amherst's actions led to what is known as "Pontiac's Rebellion," though in fact Pontiac was just one of several Ottawa chiefs. Pontiac, joined by other powerful chiefs, led a rebellion against the British. When the Indians were told they were subjects of a British king they knew was not their leader, it tipped the scales in favor of violence. Lord Amherst ordered that blankets contaminated with smallpox be sent to the tribes involved in the rebellion.

"The commander of Fort Pitt invited some of the besieging Delawares to a parley, and gave the small-pox-infected blankets from the fort hospital as a

Pontiac (standing) was an Ottawa chief who led a fight against the British colonists.

token of esteem. As the ensuing epidemic raged it progressively undermined the Indians' ability to fight, and the tide of war quickly turned against them," says historian James Wilson.[6]

Before the American Revolution, the British had set the Appalachian Mountains as the western border for their colonies. Under the Proclamation Act of 1763, white settlers were not permitted to establish homes beyond the mountains. This act confirmed the

Early Status

Indians not only taught European settlers about new crops, such as corn and squash, they also helped the settlers hunt and live in the wild new land. Intermarriage between white frontiersmen and American Indian women was common, especially in pre-Revolutionary America. Historian Landon Jones says, "Indians were originally seen not as racial inferiors but as white men in a less developed state of culture."[7]

boundary already established in the 1744 Treaty of Lancaster. Unfortunately, the pressures for more land for more people made this treaty invalid almost before it was written. There were simply not enough army officers and local laws to keep colonists from moving west past the mountains.

"The British authorities . . . unable to enforce their laws, . . . decided to rewrite them. Unable to protect Indian lands, they took them," says historian Landon Jones.[8]

In 1768 and 1784, the Iroquois sold land that they claimed to have won in battle from the Shawnee. This large tract of land includes parts of the present-day states of Kentucky, North Carolina, Georgia, South Carolina, Tennessee, and Alabama. The Shawnee were bitterly angry over this, because it included all their hunting grounds south of the Ohio River, as well as certain territories of the Cherokee.

Liberty and Justice for Some

In the aftermath of the Revolutionary War, in which the American colonists defeated Great Britain and formed the United States of America, the victorious Americans claimed that the Indians were also conquered and had to give up their lands as a consequence. The Treaty of Greenville, in 1793, gave major land grants to the Americans. "The treaty signed at Greenville was the most important Indian treaty in the nation's history," says historian Landon Jones.[9]

At the Battle of Wyoming in Pennsylvania, American Indian and Tory soldiers defeated American colonists on July 3, 1778.

The treaty and its aftermath set the stage for negotiations between American Indians and the U.S. government from then on. First, whites occupied Indian lands. The Indians would retaliate by raids on the settlements. The settlers would demand military protection. The military and the Indians would engage in battles and raids. Often starved out by having their crops destroyed and no longer having land on which to hunt or grow crops, the Indians would surrender. This surrender always meant they were coerced into giving away even more of their land.

Tecumseh and his people tried to form an alliance with other American Indians.

A sort of peace reigned in the area until two Shawnee brothers, Tecumseh and Tenskawatawa, tried to rally the scattered and saddened American Indians into an alliance they hoped would lead to peace. Fighting broke out nonetheless. As the War of 1812 led to more betrayals, fighting gradually ceased. The Indian population had decreased alarmingly, more due to disease than warfare. What would become of the rest of the American Indians?

CHAPTER Four

Indian Removal

President Thomas Jefferson had suggested the idea of a land exchange, which would mean removing the American Indians east of the Mississippi River, as early as 1802. He realized that it was going to be impossible to protect the Indians from having their land seized by state expansion. Treaty violations continued as more settlers wanted more land.

Congress did not accept the idea of removal and land exchange at that time. The Louisiana Purchase (1803), and the opening of the west through the Lewis and Clark Expedition (1804–1806), created a vast new area for expansion. After the end of the War of 1812, the idea of a land exchange was again considered. By then, the boundary had been pushed farther west than the Appalachian Mountains. "A Permanent Indian Territory in the newly acquired territory between the Mississippi and the Rocky Mountains now appeared to be the ideal solution to the Indian problem in the East," says geographer Klaus Franz.[1]

The Bureau of Indian Affairs

In 1824, a bill signed by Secretary of War John C. Calhoun created a Bureau of Indian Affairs. The first superintendent of the bureau, Thomas L. McKenney, realized that removal was the only policy that northeastern settlers would tolerate. He made statements that indicated that if Indians were not removed from the northeast, they would quickly face extinction.[2]

The Permanent Indian Territory that had opened up west of the Alleghenies and especially in the territory of the Louisiana Purchase, had a major complication. It happened to be the homeland of many other American Indian nations who had always lived in the west. What was to be done with these other Indians? And, what problems would it cause for the unwilling intruders, such as the Cherokee, to be seen as invading someone else's territory?

This had crossed the minds of the settlers familiar with the Indians along the Missouri River, who were having their own difficulties living near the existing American Indians. During the first few years of American independence, the new government made peace treaties with American Indians in outlying areas. These peace treaties were always written in ways that ensured large chunks of land would go to the white settlers. However, there was still an option for large Indian nations, such as the Delaware of the northeast coast, or the Cherokee in the southeast, to either join the union as a state or to remain a sovereign nation.

The Cherokee and related nations in the South realized, after the American Revolution, that further resistance to the white invaders was impossible. Most of the tribes—even the powerful Muskogee, also called the Creek—tried to create governments that were similar to the newly created American republic. The Cherokee used the American example to set up a constitution as a sovereign nation. The colonists in the state of Georgia, despite the Cherokee's decision to never again sell any of their land, simply declared their constitution invalid. Georgia then divided up the Cherokee's land into separate counties of the state.

The Cherokee were saddened and angered by the realization that no matter what they did or how well they succeeded in living the same as the white settlers, they would always be viewed as inferior. They had hoped that treaty obligations would protect them, but the constant hunger for land from increasing numbers of settlers signaled the final stage of the American Indian removal policy: reservations.

Cherokee Nation v. State of Georgia

The Cherokee went to the new United States Supreme Court to object to the takeover of their land. In a famous court case, called *Cherokee Nation* v. *State of Georgia, 1831*, the court ruled that yes, the Cherokee and other American Indian groups were foreign nations, but since they occupied land in the United States they were actually "domestic dependents" and the court therefore felt it was not able to rule in the case.

The Trail of Tears

The first reservations were simply areas of land called territories, to which American Indians were transported. The term "Trail of Tears" specifically refers to the 1838 march of fifteen thousand Cherokee during which four thousand people died from starvation, disease, and brutal weather conditions.[3] However, the larger Trail of Tears was the actual Indian Removal Act of 1830, which led to ten years of brutal marches. During this time about sixty thousand individuals from Cherokee, Chickasaw, Choctaw, Creek, and Seminole nations were removed from their southeastern homes and sent to the Indian Territory.[4] This number becomes higher when other relocations, totaling some sixty Indian groups, is included.[5]

This territory set aside for relocation was defined as being west of the Mississippi and not in the states of Missouri, Louisiana, or the territory of

The painting The Trail of Tears *by Robert Lindneux depicts the mass forced movement of the Cherokee to Indian Territory in present-day Oklahoma.*

Arkansas. President Andrew Jackson signed the Indian Removal Act in violation of a U.S. Supreme Court case (*Worcester* v. *Georgia*) under Chief Justice John Marshall, which held that state laws could not be enforced on American Indian lands. When informed of this legal decision, Jackson replied, "John Marshall has made his decision. Now let him enforce it!"[6]

In the area around St. Louis, Missouri, nations such as the Osage and the Kansas had to be dealt

Forced Movement

"Enforcement" of removal policies often meant brutal force. Author Peter Nabokov, referring to collected narratives of both Indians and whites involved in the removal to Indian Territory, wrote:

> Families at dinner were startled by the sudden gleam of bayonets in the doorway and rose up to be driven with blows amid oaths along the trail that led to the stockade. Men were seized in their fields or going along the road, women were taken from their spinning wheels and children from their play.[7]

with before full-scale removal could take place. William Clark, Superintendent of Indian Affairs, was charged with handling the Indians who might be in the way of eastern tribes emigrating west. William Clark noted in his logbook, during September 1826, that members of the Shawnee, Potawatomi, Kickapoo, Delaware, Osage, and Peoria nations applied to him for provisions to move west.[8]

By the end of 1827, it was hard to keep up with the needs for food and clothing for the large numbers of Indians whose lands had been confiscated and who had no way to make a living. "The tribes on this side of the Mississippi are wretched and moving from place to place . . . the distresses of the Indians of this Superintendency are so great and extensive, and complaints so frequent, it is, and has been impossible for me to report them. I therefore have taken upon myself a great deal, in acting as I thought best."[9] Clark was not the only American who was outraged by the treatment of the Indians—though he seems to have shared the majority opinion that removal was the only way to save them from extinction.

Before this increasing number of American Indians moving west could even get started on the trail, smallpox again struck their people. Reports were that at least half of the people in the nations on the lower Missouri had died. But in Washington, the War Department was more interested in reports on the fur trade than on this tragedy.

The unwilling immigrants to the plains area designated as Indian Territory, which was also labeled The Great American Desert or Permanent

In addition to the Cherokee, other Indians were forced to move West, often through harsh conditions.

Making a New Life

The Cherokee and other tribes who did make it alive to Indian Territory were only beginning their hardship. Basically farmers, they had trouble growing enough food on land that had never before been plowed and was often not suitable. The government did not send the equipment and seeds they had promised. Other nations, such as the Comanche, Kiowa, and Pawnee, who were already there, were hunters whose major food source was the buffalo. They resented this invasion into their territory. Nations who had cooperated in the past became rivals.

Indian Country, tried valiantly to start their lives anew. The Indian Appropriation Act of 1851 formed official reservations from the territories occupied by the dislodged eastern nations. Already reservations had been set aside in the south and northwest.

Soon, powerful forces, including gold strikes in the formerly Spanish-held southwest and California, and farther north in Oregon territory, would again take homes away from this devastated culture. Perhaps if it had not been for the gold strikes in California, the huge surge of migration to what had appeared to be desert and mountainous country too difficult to cross would not have happened. As author Nabokov reports, between 1849 and 1852, the gold rush sent one hundred seventy-five thousand people storming west, right through Indian Territory.[10]

CHAPTER Five

Setting the Stage for Reservations

The discovery of gold in California in 1848 began to attract miners, settlers, and the eastern American Indians already removed to the Western territories. However, even before the huge migration caused by the gold rush, Indians in what are now the northwestern and southwestern United States were affected. Indians along the Santa Fe trade routes were becoming aggressive as their homelands were invaded and game became scarce. In the Rocky Mountains, the constant hunting for furs had depleted game. Between 1800 and 1840, three smallpox pandemics had devastating effects on many of the Plains Indians.

Steamboats had been going up and down the Missouri River since 1818. An effort had been made

Broken Treaties

"Of all Indian regions in America, California, with its medley of different native groups peopling diverse eco-regions, suffered the most after the United States won these lands from Mexico," says author Peter Nabokov.[1] Eighteen Indian groups were talked into signing treaties for reservations, but there were so many objections from white settlers at giving Indians any land that could possibly be used for agriculture and mining that the treaties were never honored. Instead, the government rewarded "volunteer armies" who wiped out entire Indian villages, so that by 1853 there was no land that belonged to Indians. After the Gold Rush, nations that had numbered four thousand to fourteen thousand had only a few, struggling survivors.[2]

in 1832 to inoculate the Western Indian tribes against the repeated outbreaks of smallpox. Unfortunately, the efforts stopped before the doctors reached the Mandan, the Arikara, the Assiniboine, and the Cree.

More Disease

In 1837, the steamboat called the St. Peters carried a passenger who came down with smallpox. The ensuing epidemic killed many members of the nations that had been visited by the Lewis and Clark expedition. The Mandan Indians, whose nation was already affected by smallpox, numbered about sixteen hundred in early 1837. By the end of that year, there were only thirty-one Mandan left. More than half of the Arikara Indians died. The Cree, with about three thousand tribal members, and the Assiniboines, who had numbered ten thousand, were almost completely wiped out.[3] The Blackfeet in the Rocky Mountains were the next to be affected. Only the Lakota Sioux, off on a buffalo hunt in the far reaches of their territory, came out of this particular epidemic with little harm, according to Landon Jones.[4]

Bureau of Indian Affairs agent Joshua Pilcher wrote to William Clark that "The country through which [the smallpox epidemic] has passed is literally depopulated and converted into one great grave-yard."[5] In an effort to find the Lakota Sioux and inoculate them, Clark and Pilcher hired a doctor, Joseph R. De Prefontaine, to give vaccinations. About three thousand Indians were vaccinated as the steamboat stopped along the Missouri River. The Lakota Sioux were never reached, due to the doctor's own illness.

Settling the West

By 1850, the United States had managed to rid itself of all European territorial claims from the Atlantic Ocean to the Pacific Ocean. The only obstacle to complete settlement of the West were the American Indian nations, many of whom had been already reduced by disease, alcohol, and hunger. Because of the large numbers of people migrating through their territory, the Plains Indians became the next to be affected by settlers moving west.

The Plains Indians, with the possible exception of the Blackfeet confederacy, did not have the unity of the Iroquois nations. The Plains Indians had become swift riders after European explorers introduced them to horses. Hunting game, especially buffalo, was a way of life, and highly territorial. As the game disappeared, Plains Indians were forced to move farther from their homes to hunt. This encroachment strained relations between nations and led to warfare.

Throughout the 1830s and 1840s, the Cheyenne and Arapaho fought the Comanche and the Kiowa; the Sioux and the Northern Cheyenne were at war with the Crow. All of these nations threatened the Shoshone and the Pawnee. The Delaware, Shawnee, Potawatomi, and other smaller nations, who had been removed to Indian Territory, fought for their own space on the plains. Into this warfare came white settlers, hungry for their own land.

Some Indian groups formed war parties to attack settlers' wagon trains. Raiding parties stole cows and horses from the settlers, and the government stepped in. Of the fifty-six military posts in the United States in 1845, twenty-four of them were west of the Mississippi. In 1849, two forts were set up

The Sioux were one of the groups of Plains Indians. This painting by George Catlin shows a Sioux camp on the upper Missouri River.

along the Laramie River in Wyoming, and two years later a great council of the northern nations was held at nearby Horse Creek. The number of Indians who attended this council is estimated to be ten thousand.[6]

Nations who had never met each other except in war camped together at Horse Creek and agreed to a general peace. Assiniboine, Atsina, Arikara, Crow, Shoshone, Sioux, Cheyenne, and Arapaho agreed not to attack the wagon trains that surged through their land. In exchange, the United States promised to use its troops to protect the Indians from whites, who stole their land and attacked their villages. Two years later, in 1853, the United States made the same promises to the Comanche, Kiowa, and other southern Plains Indians. As settlers spilled across the plains, the promises fell away. The troops began a series of Indian wars, attacking the same nations they had promised to protect.

Indian Appropriations Act

In 1854, Congress passed the Indian Appropriations Act. This legalized the formation of Indian reservations and the removal of designated tribes to specific locations. Not only the Plains Indians were affected; the Pueblo, Navajo, Ute, and Apache were removed to reservations. In Texas, the native Apache, Kiowa, and Comanche were relocated to two small reservations.

In the Northwest, the Yakima signed a treaty giving away 10 million acres of their land for the promise of government supplies and support. Not all their chiefs agreed to this and battles raged for three years. However, after fighting valiantly to save their land, the remaining Yakima were confined to a small reservation in the eastern part of the state. The Blackfeet also signed a treaty that reduced their territory. In all, fifty-two treaties, which forced

What is a Reservation?

The word "reservation" has more than one meaning. *Webster's New World Dictionary*'s second definition is "a public land set aside for some special use."[7] The *Oxford Compact English Dictionary* is even more specific: "an area of land set aside for occupation by North American Indians or Australian Aboriginals."[8]

western Indians to live on a small amount of their former territory, were in place by 1856.

Cherokee Land

Those Cherokee who survived the Trail of Tears and the first difficult years in a harsh land had prospered. The more they succeeded with housing, agriculture, and self-governance, the more settlers wanted the land on which they lived. Because the Cherokee and other relocated nations had retained their belief that all their citizens had a right to land—which was held by each nation and not by individuals—the entire population prospered. This only fueled the desire of land speculators to take over the land on which the Cherokee had done so well. "In the presidential election campaign of 1860, William Seward publicly declared that: "'Indian Territory south of Kansas must be vacated by the Indian,'" says historian James Wilson.[9]

Without the Civil War, perhaps the Cherokee might have been able to keep this land and become an

Plains Indians

After the Plains Indians began using horses, they grew more nomadic as hunting became possible in a wider territory. As other Indian groups were dwindling, the Plains Indians' population grew. By 1800, the Plains included thirty different Indian groups. It was not until 1837 that disease killed many of these American Indians. Almost all of these American Indians rode horses. These societies spoke six different languages.[10]

example for other confined tribes. However, the unity of their government collapsed after both the Union and the Confederacy offered empty promises.

The Cherokee were not the only nation adversely affected by the Civil War, which began in 1861. In the early months of the war, the U.S. government withdrew almost all its troops from the Plains. This meant that there were fewer American Indian attacks on wagon trains, "suggesting that, left to themselves, the supposedly bloodthirsty Sioux and other tribes were prepared to co-exist peacefully . . . and were more interested in hunting than in killing Americans," says Wilson.[11]

Further Suffering

This small reprieve was not to last. By 1862, Indians in the Northwest, having had their land and their game taken away, were suffering from hunger. The annuity payments to the Indians, which paid for the meager supplies handed out to the reservation Indians, had been reallocated to the war effort. For the Santee Sioux, who had given up nine-tenths of their territory so they could feed their people (and settlers were already encroaching on the small area they had left), it was the last straw. Bureau of Indian Affairs agent, Thomas Galbraith, refused to distribute the food without the annuity money. Gathering at the agency, the Santee chief, Ta-oya-te-duta (Little Crow), gave this speech:

> We have waited a long time. The money is ours, but we cannot get it. We have no food, but here are these stores, filled with food. We ask that you, the agent, make some arrangement by which we can get food from the stores, or else we may take our own way to keep ourselves from starving. When men are hungry they help themselves.[12]

Shortly after this, the Santee revolted, attacking the agency and settlers. The U.S. government, despite waging a war on the Confederacy, sent soldiers and volunteer frontiersmen to fight the Indians. This action began the series of battles called the Indian Wars, which would soon be romanticized as "The Wild West."

CHAPTER Six

How the West Was Won

"We had a good country until the white people came and crowded us . . . My ancestors were glad to see the white strangers come . . . my people made no trouble, although the whites killed many of them! Only when they want to put us in one small place, taking from us our home country, trouble started."

Hemene Moxmox (Yellow Wolf), of the Nez Perce nation[1]

From 1860 to 1891, there were more than a thousand armed conflicts between American Indians and whites in the Plains region. It was an era of bloody battles in which the Indian population fought valiantly to retain their land, customs, and very existence. Already destroyed by disease and alcoholism, hungry and cold, the Plains Indian leaders fought the inevitable end of their civilization.

Railroads crossed their former hunting grounds as train passengers even leaned out of windows to shoot at the diminishing herds of buffalo.

In the Southwest, the Navajo and Apache raided settlements not so much for food as to rescue their women and children who had been enslaved. "It was officially estimated that 2,000 Indian slaves were held by the white people of New Mexico and Arizona in 1866," says historian William Brandon.[2] This was a particular problem for the Apache, whose famous chiefs Cochise and Mangas Coloradas managed in 1861 to temporarily rid Arizona of most of its white people.

Apache and the Navajo

These Apache, also called the Mescaleros, were the first to be sent to an arid, desert reservation at Bosque Redondo, in the Pecos River Valley. Indian fighter Kit Carson, boasting that "wild Indians could be tamed,"[3] conquered the Navajo by entering Canyon de Chelly, where they lived and farmed. His troops burned their hogans (houses), orchards, and fields, and seized their livestock. The Navajo, starving and bewildered, were driven on the "Long Walk" to Bosque Redondo. Many died of disease and starvation in that dry and desolate landscape. Four years later, the Navajo were allowed to return to a portion of their former land. They were given thirty-five thousand sheep and goats to promote sheepherding.

Famous Names

The era of Indian wars gave names to specific battles that have entered Western folklore. Fallen Timbers, Horseshoe Bend, Little Big Horn, Chief Joseph's War, and the Pequot War are the most famous. Even better known are the massacres: at Wounded Knee, of Californian Indians, of Cheyenne at Sand Creek, at Taos and at Tolowas. Indian names such as Sitting Bull, Cochise, Chief Joseph, Little Crow, Quana Parker, Red Cloud, Geronimo, and Crazy Horse are famous for their armed resistance to white domination.

This began a cycle of industriousness and adaptation to life. Their excellent weaving and silver jewelry-making would become a moderate success story in the future.

The Nez Perce

The Nez Perce were superb horsemen who brought many warriors to a treaty council at Walla Walla, Washington, in 1855. There they agreed to a reduction in their territory that became the Nez Perce reservation. However, by 1860, when gold was discovered in Oregon, settlers overwhelmed the Wallowa Valley which was at the center of the Nez Perce reservation. Led by a chief called Old Joseph, the Nez Perce became known for a policy of passive resistance. They stayed on their land despite the abuses of their white "neighbors."

In 1873, the U.S. government proclaimed the Wallowa Valley a reservation—for the second time. It had been proclaimed by a treaty already. This did not stop the settlers from murdering American Indians whenever they could. Three years later, in one more stunning reversal of a promise, the Nez Perce were told they had thirty days to move their people to Idaho. To not comply would be an act of war. By this time, Old Joseph had died and Young Joseph was the chief. He and a chief named Ollokut tried to negotiate peace terms while hiding their people. Finally, carrying a flag of truce, a group of U.S. soldiers fired into a group of Nez Perce, who returned fire.

Chief Joseph marched his people seventeen hundred miles, winning skirmishes with the army repeatedly. He insisted that no killing would happen that was not defensive. Most of the other chiefs died along the way, and many of the Nez Perce starved as winter arrived. Just thirty miles from the safety of the Canadian border, Chief Joseph was forced to surrender. He and others of his tribe who refused to give up their beliefs spent the rest of their lives on the Colville reservation in Washington State's most dry region.

American Indian Victories

The massive migration to the Western states by white settlers continued. Military pursuit to subdue

Chief Joseph led the Nez Perce in a fight against U.S. troops.

Words of Surrender

Chief Joseph's words as he surrendered have become famous as the speech of an extraordinary human being:

> I am tired of fighting. Our chiefs are killed . . . The old men are all dead. It is cold and we have no blankets. The little children are freezing to death. My people, some of them, have run away to the hills, and have no blankets, no food; no one knows where they are— perhaps freezing to death. I want to have time to look for my children and see how many I can find. Maybe I shall find them among the dead. Hear me, my chiefs. I am tired; my heart is sick and sad. From where the sun now stands I will fight no more forever.[4]

the outraged Indians cost the government millions of dollars and many dead soldiers. Most of the battles during this period occurred because Indians who had been confined to a reservation on a small portion of their former land refused to stay there. They were starving—at least if they left the reservation they might be able to hunt the now scarce animals. And, the reservation boundaries kept changing as white settlers found even those lands desirable.

The Lakota Sioux, led by Chief Red Cloud, not only defeated the army on many occasions, but attacked the various forts along the Bozeman trail. Staggering under the expense of these wars, the government signed yet another treaty at Fort Laramie, in 1868, and agreed to close the Bozeman trail and

Chief Red Cloud led a series of attacks against American forts.

Northwest Ordinance

The Northwest Ordinance of 1787 read in part:

The utmost good faith shall always be observed towards the Indians; their lands and property shall never be taken without their consent; and in their property, rights, and liberty, they shall never be invaded or disturbed, unless in just and lawful wars authorized by Congress; but laws founded in justice and humility shall from time to time be made for preventing wrongs being done to them, and for preserving peace and friendship with them.[5]

leave western South Dakota as unconquered Indian territory.

This Indian victory had little impact on the bad treatment of American Indians. In 1871, the U.S. government simply decided to stop making treaties. There would be no more treating the Indians as independent nations, but instead the goal was to get them onto reservations as quickly as possible. There they would be completely dependent on government support and rations, and perhaps could be educated.

One of the voices for making Indians wards of the government and for treating them fairly on the reservations was the Commissioner of Indian Affairs, Ely S. Parker. He was a Seneca Indian who had risen to power during the administration of President Ulysses S. Grant. Highly intelligent and motivated to succeed, Parker received his law degree and then a degree in civil engineering. He faced much discrimination when he tried to use his knowledge and skills to make a place for himself in white society, but he believed that there was no choice for Indians but to become educated in the white man's ways of life.[6]

This view of what should now be done with the Indians who were rapidly losing their lands, was at odds with other views that called for extermination. Colonel John Gibbon won a gold medal for an essay in an Army competition, writing:

> Philanthropists and visionary speculators may theorize as they please about protecting the Indian . . . and preserving him as a race. It cannot be done. Whenever the two come in contact . . . the weaker must give way, and disappear. To deny this is to deny the evidence of our own senses, and to shut our eyes to the facts of history.[7]

Opposed to this view were those who had been outraged by the reports of the Sand Creek Massacre, in 1864. The Cheyenne Indians, "after living on government rations at Fort Lyon for a while . . . were instructed to shift their camp to Sand Creek, some thirty miles from the military post, where they could hunt for themselves," says historian Peter Nabokov.[8] Instead, the Cheyenne, as well as the Arapaho camped with them, became the hunted. Seven hundred troops, in early dawn, fired on the sleeping camp and killed all they could find, "babies and mothers, warriors and grandparents."[9] Chief Black Kettle took what was left of his people and camped as far away from troops as he could. Four years after Sand Creek, Colonel George Armstrong Custer, in his first Indian battle, attacked the camp with his seventh cavalry, and massacred forty more of the Cheyenne. In 1870, troops descended on a Blackfeet camp in Montana, "leaving 173 men, women and children dead in the snow," according to Nabokov.[10] The next year in Arizona, 85 Apache, mostly women and children, were killed by settlers in what came to be known as the Camp Grant Massacre.

There was to be one more massive Indian war and one more massacre, among the many small skirmishes and atrocities that marked the late nineteenth century in the West. The Battle of the Little Big Horn, on June 25, 1876, which resulted from yet another reduction in hunting grounds for the Sioux, was a major defeat for the U.S. Army. Sitting Bull and Crazy Horse led a force of nearly two thousand warriors, the largest assembly of Indian forces ever gathered on the Plains. It took the Indians just one hour to wipe out Custer's company of 210 soldiers, and not much longer to almost wipe out soldiers from a following company.

Though this was a major victory for the Sioux, the shock of the complete loss of a company and its leader set the stage for a massive upsurge in military pursuit of all the Indians in the area. As the Indians were rounded up and sent to reservations, punishment in the form of reduced food and clothing rations was common. Soldiers who were frightened by his presence murdered Chief Crazy Horse, after his surrender.[11]

This depiction of the Battle of the Little Bighorn was painted by Amos Bad Heart Bull, an Oglala Sioux from the Pine Ridge Reservation.

The Disappearing American Indian

When the treaty policy ended in 1871, 370 treaties, beginning in 1778, had been agreed upon between the U.S. government American Indians. The majority of those treaties were violated, not by the Indians, but by the whites. The idea that American Indians were considered sovereign peoples, with power to negotiate treaties, had ended, with horrendous consequences for America's original inhabitants.

Indians on reservations were included for the first time in the 1890 census. By that year, the population of the United States was 63 million. The Indian population, estimated at around 5 million in 1600, was only two hundred thirty-seven thousand. George L. Russell, writer, demographer, and a Saginaw Chippewa wrote: "In fewer than one hundred years, Indian tribal lands had been reduced [from] all land west of the Appalachian Mountains to desolate reservations totaling less than four percent of the continental United States."[12]

CHAPTER *Seven*

Violence and Betrayal

The complete disrespect for the land, lives, and cultural beliefs of the American Indian population caused great upheaval in communities and untold personal suffering. Indian spiritual beliefs had always been a part of every day, of everything from hunting to communal ritual. In order to bring some sense back to their world, various tribes looked for spiritual guidance and help, often combining Christian beliefs with their old ways of spiritual connection.

Turning to Religion

Wovoka, a Paiute prophet, preached a message of hope that included prayer, rejection of alcohol, and ceremonial purification as the way to bring back the

The Ghost Dance

George Sword, an Ogalala Sioux, describes the Ghost Dance as follows:

> The persons in the ghost dancing all joined hands. A man stands and then a woman, so in that way forming a very large circle. They dance around in the circle in a continuous time until some of them become so tired and overtired that they became crazy and finally drop as though dead.[1]

old way of life. Do not mourn, he said, the future can have hope. There will be a future that brings back the buffalo and without white men in it to harm you.[2]

The major component of the ceremonial purification was the Ghost Dance. Indians from across the Plains, particularly the Sioux, Cheyenne, and Arapaho, came together to sing and sway, wearing special "ghost" shirts that were supposed to make them safe against bullets. The dance allowed them to enter trances in which they experienced a happier future.

White settlers knew of this Ghost Dance and became alarmed by the idea of American Indians dancing wildly and talking of the disappearance of white men. Searching for the leaders of this spiritual movement, agents of the Bureau of Indian Affairs killed Sitting Bull and seven ghost dancers. Word, and alarm, spread among the Indians and the whites. The revitalization of spiritual movements, such as the Ghost Dance, led to the tragedy at Wounded Knee.

A Horrible Massacre

A Sioux leader named Big Foot led his followers, which included around four hundred men, women, and children, to the Pine Ridge reservation. Their purpose was to arrange a meeting with other Sioux leaders.

On December 28, 1890, the seventh cavalry, with five hundred soldiers, met Big Foot's group, who were ordered to camp at Wounded Knee creek. The next morning all the Sioux men were told to line up and give up their weapons. "As a deaf Sioux called Black Coyote was struggling to hold on to his rifle a shot was heard (it is still not clear which side it came from) and the nervous cavalry opened fire," says James Wilson.[3]

One of Big Foot's warriors who survived the massacre was Wasumaza (who later changed his name to Dewey Beard). He gave an eye witness account of the beginning of the slaughter. His account appears in *Bury My Heart At Wounded Knee*, by Dee Brown:

> If they had left him [Black Coyote] alone he was going to put his gun down where he should . . . He hadn't his gun pointed at anyone. . . . They came on and grabbed the gun that he was going to put down. Right after they spun him around there was the report of a gun, quite loud.[4]

Because of the cavalry's powerful rapid-fire weapons called Hotchkiss guns, the Sioux men were killed immediately. The soldiers continued to fire as

Bodies of Sioux Indians are unceremoniously piled into a mass grave hacked into the frozen South Dakota soil after the tragedy at Wounded Knee.

some Indians fought back with whatever they had at hand and others tried to run away. About two hundred people were killed within an hour and others were pursued by the soldiers as they fled. Around one hundred made it to the nearby hills where they later froze to death.

According to Peter Nabokov, though the massacre at Wounded Knee might have been the *coup de grace* (or final blow) to large-scale Indian rebellion and peaceful protest in the nineteenth century, other forces were more devastating. "The devastation wrought by disease and the expropriation of their land through the bloodless process of treaty making and anti-Indian legislation" were the major causes of loss of freedom for all the tribes.[5]

The Dawes Act

The Dawes Act, or the General Allotment Act passed in 1887, created more pressure for American Indian lands and contributed to the climate in which incidents like Wounded Knee could occur. Ever since white settlers came to North America and began wanting to own specific parcels of land, they had looked down on the Indian notion of using land in common. The concept of private ownership of land was completely foreign to Indians, who believed that land was not something to be owned. Though certain areas were considered tribal hunting territories, this was far different from individual "ownership" of a piece of the earth. Europeans simply did not understand, and certainly did not respect, the idea of a group of people who spoke of land as "ours."

Dividing land into plots owned by a single family was popular with a wide variety of people, with a variety of interests. People who felt the only way to "save" the Indians was to make them act like everybody else, with the same customs and daily lives as white people, thought single-plot ownership was the key. The Bureau of Indian Affairs thought it could reduce the bill for food and services required by former treaties on the reservations. They also knew they could profit by selling whatever reservation land was left after the single-plot subdivision. Even Indians who had managed to have some power in the white world, including Indian commissioner Ely Parker, believed that private land ownership would help Indians gain a higher standard of living than seemed possible at that time.

But there were many pitfalls in this argument. First, there was no guarantee as to the quality of land taken from the common reservation. Many of these reservations were located on dry soil that could not support agriculture. And if it was good land, what was to stop the constant land hunger that sent settlers surging through Indian lands? What was to stop these private plots from falling into the hands of land speculators who offered to buy them from hungry, discouraged Indians?

The Indian population had shrunk alarmingly over the years. But if families were settled on small private plots, and if the death rate from murder, disease, and hunger was reduced, there might be more Indians, not fewer. No one considered that, if allotment brought about the improved conditions

Poor Land

Most of the allotment land was not good for small farming. "A Kiowa chief acidly observed that if the President was so eager to have the Indians raise corn, he should send them land that would grow corn," notes historian Ralph K. Andrist.[6]

for Indians that it was supposed to, the Indian population might increase. In the Great Lakes region an allotment was 80 acres and sometimes only 40 acres. In the West the land allotment was 160 acres and occasionally 320 acres. What would happen to those plots of land when they had to be divided among the heirs—children and grandchildren—of the families who owned them? They would, of course, become smaller and smaller and, not very gradually, would become too small to support the families who farmed them.

Some Indians accepted allotment as inevitable, whether they believed it would be beneficial to them or not. "Many tribes, however, put up stiff resistance." says historian James Wilson.[7] Southwestern nations asked for help from the better organized groups like the Cherokee, Chickasaw, Choctaw, Creek, Seminole, and the Osage, whose lands—still not being called a reservation—were not part of the allotment plan. A committee of twenty-two Indian nations met to try to unite as one Indian government to fight allotment.

The committee set about drafting a constitution for an Indian Union. However, before it could meet again, the U.S. government had forced the sale of two million acres of land belonging to the Cherokee, Chickasaw, Choctaw, Creek, and Seminole nations. The next year, their former land was reorganized as Oklahoma Territory, open to white settlement. The Cherokee and other tribes were forced onto a small part of their former lands, their successful farms and schools closed.

In other areas, resistance was less obvious, but the discontent was apparent to white settlers. In the Northwest, the Commissioner of Indian Affairs ordered that no Indians leave the reservation without permission. If too much grumbling occurred, the Bureau of Indian affairs withheld government food, clothing, and other supplies, on which the tribes had become dependent. And if there was more trouble, the army could be called in to subdue protest. The growing strength of the Ghost Dance movement, which preceded the massacre at Wounded Knee, occurred during resistance to the Dawes Act.

Surplus land, that is land that once was part of a reservation, was put up for sale to white settlers. "This action was in direct violation of the treaty agreements," says Indian author George Russell. "Prior to the Allotment Act tribal land holdings totaled 138 million acres. By the end of the allotment period in 1934, nearly 90 million acres held passed

Broken Trust

Often American Indians avoided confrontation by retreating into areas that seemed unwanted by white settlers. There they could continue to live at least somewhat according to their own customs. The White River Utes left their reservation and headed for South Dakota. The Kickapoo in western Indian Territory, when faced with dividing their reservation into allotments, gave all their money to a lawyer who promised to buy them land in Mexico. He, and several other government figures, including a senator, took the money and never purchased land. This left the Kickapoo in great poverty and forced them to accept the allotment system.

out of Indian tribal ownership."[8] Massive land transfers occurred through lotteries, sealed bids, and "runs," something that became famous in Western movies. Anyone wanting to stake a claim to former Indian land could start at a fixed point, in a wagon or on a horse or mule, and "run" to claim land. Two million acres of treaty-held Indian lands were confiscated using this method.

In 1890, former Cherokee and other American Indian lands in present-day Oklahoma became home to sixty thousand whites. Ten years later, the white population was four hundred thousand. By 1890, the government acquired 13 million acres; by 1891, 23 million acres; by 1892, 30 million acres—all former reservation land.[9]

Land Lost

Historian Peter Nabokov explains the progression of land loss:

> An astonishing amount of land had been transferred from Indian to white control by the close of the nineteenth century. Through treaties, purchases, and outright theft, claim to the continent was wrested from the native peoples. Today, many native Americans are trying to reclaim lands that were illegally expropriated in the past.[10]

The Dawes Act allowed for a phenomenon known as checker-boarding, or mixed land ownership. Land on many reservations came to look like a checkerboard, with land owned by Indian individuals, non-Indian individuals or groups, the state, the county, and the federal government. According to the treaties that created the reservations, all land within the boundaries of the reservation was supposed to be owned by the American Indians settled there.

It was not only the loss of land that was caused by allotment. The idea of lands parceled out to individuals who were then expected to farm them in the white man's way, changed age-old cultural practices. Reservations were each assigned to a Christian denomination and Indian religious rituals were suppressed, often violently.

As Charlotte Black Elk, Lakota Sioux says:

> All of a sudden we were told: Not only will you not be able to practice your religion, but you shall also bring all of your sacred objects—sacred pipes, spirit

White settlers rush to claim land in what would become Oklahoma Territory in September 1893.

bundles, everything that we had that was sacred—into the agency and there we shall have a grand bonfire. Every little thing that told us we were Lakota and that was tied into our culture, our social fabric, was outlawed. [These practices were designed to say] everything about you is bad. So everything about our culture was systematically to be destroyed.[11]

As destructive as allotment was, the breaking up of families due to the formation of American Indian boarding schools caused the most alienation of Indians, from each other, and from themselves.

CHAPTER Eight

Indian Schools and Early Life on Reservations

As early as 1879, the idea of American Indian schools entered the reservation system. Individual ownership of land was one thing, but what the American government thought really needed to happen was the education of the Indian in the exact same way as white children. However, this education would not stop at English grammar and mathematics. Before this could happen, the children would be forced to not speak their native tongue and to give up the long hair and loose (and comfortable) dress of their people.

American Indian Schools

The first Indian school, which became a model for others, was the Carlisle Indian School in Pennsylvania. It was founded by Captain Richard Pratt, who believed that Indian children needed to achieve an entirely new identity. In one of his many pro-nouncements, he stated his major aim in this slogan, "Kill the Indian and save the man!"[1] Though Pratt was not among the many whites who believed that American Indians were an inferior race who deserved to be killed, he believed that everything about their culture must be destroyed in order to "civilize" the children he and others would teach.

When children arrived at the school they had their hair cut very short or often had their heads shaved. They put on uncomfortable uniforms and tight-waisted dresses and were marched in military drill. They were given English names. They were forbidden to speak their own language, and severely punished, sometimes beaten and disfigured, if they forgot to speak English.

The food was perhaps one of the most difficult adjustments. In some schools, instead of simple meat and soup and some vegetables, they were fed a diet of white bread, coffee, and sugar. This poor diet, coupled with tuberculosis, influenza, and other ailments, caused the death of many Indian children. At the end of the first three years at the Carlisle Indian School, "nearly one half of the children from the Plains were dead and through with all earthly schools. In the graveyard at Carlisle most of the graves were those of little ones," remembers Luther Standing Bear, one of the first Carlisle pupils.[2]

These photos show Tom Torlino before and after he started attending Carlisle Indian School.

Publicity about the school painted a very different picture than the true one of suffering. Educating Indian children became a popular occupation for teachers from many different Christian faiths. Since breaking down the culture was thought to be an important part of assimilation, most of these schools were boarding schools where the parents were not allowed to visit.

A few families were successful at hiding their children so that they never entered the degrading system. Many children forced to enter the schools ran away and were severely punished when they were caught and returned. Thousands of children died from diet and disease, and some children seemed to just waste away from loneliness. Some children ended up becoming good students, and entering the white man's world, where they faced discrimination in employment. Others were able to bring their learning back to their people and still respect the old ways. Most of those who survived, however, were confused as to which culture to embrace.

Life on the Early Reservations

What about the reservations these Indian children were taken from? How did these formerly independent, strong, and community-minded people live at the end of the nineteenth century and the early years of the twentieth century?

To fully understand what the reservations were like, it is necessary to review the relatively short history of American Indian/European relations in the United States.

The progression to total dependence on the government had three phases. In the first years after the Revolutionary War, Indian groups were recognized as sovereign nations. For instance, the United States and the Iroquois Confederacy, existed side by side as equal powers. As more and more land was taken away from American Indians, they began to be considered domestic dependent nations, no longer an equal power. If the United States had other nations living within it, then it became the responsibility of the government to protect the members of those nations. The treaties made with these nations were always broken. (This became important in the twentieth century because treaties are legal documents, and American Indians began to seek legal enforcement of old treaties.)

Finally, the whole idea of separate nations disappeared as the land owned and lived on by Indians became smaller. The Plains Indians could no longer feed themselves because the buffalo were gone (by 1900 there were thirty-nine buffalo in Yellowstone National Park)[3] and the land used for all game hunting was filled with settlers.

An example of how the land for reservations was whittled away is what happened to the Western Sioux. Their original reservation was designated as all of South Dakota west of the Mississippi River. They also had treaty-negotiated hunting rights in Montana and Wyoming. When gold was discovered in the Black Hills of South Dakota, the government offered to buy the area from the Sioux. When they refused, they were forced onto the reservation. The Battle of the Little Big Horn followed.

Pursued relentlessly after their victory, the Sioux ended up by losing a full third of their reservation and all their hunting rights in Montana and Wyoming. The next reduction came when settlers complained to the government about the Sioux

Four Lakota Sioux women stand with a Lakota man on horseback on the Pine Ridge Reservation in South Dakota.

reservation being in the way of their emigration to eastern Dakota. The Sioux were then forced to create a sixty-mile-wide corridor right through the middle and the farthest western portion of their reservation. The remainder was divided up into the five small reservations they occupy today. And that was not all—the Dawes Act was enacted and the remaining reservation was divided into 160-acre parcels and what was left over was sold to whites.[4]

On the Sioux and almost all other reservations, Indians had no way to work or hunt for their own food.

Many reservations had rules that would not allow American Indians to leave the boundaries. The reservation Indians became totally dependent on government rations. They lost a sense of purpose, hope, and self esteem and were reduced often to begging and petty stealing just to fill their stomachs. They suffered tuberculosis and other diseases, malnutrition, and alcoholism. The government rations were often cut in half or replaced with spoiled food and shoddy goods because of widespread corruption among officials and agents employed by the Bureau of Indian Affairs. Though there were a few good and honest agents, they were often removed because the middlemen who supplied the reservations wanted to continue to put the money in their own pockets.

Poverty

Reservations became places of chronic poverty, with no work available. "In the decade after the Civil War, behind-the-scenes corruption in the Indian Bureau went from bad to worse," says Nabokov.[5] Members of Congress, dishonest suppliers of the food and other goods, and Indian agents often came up with schemes to divert the money owed to the reservations.

In 1867, a group of citizens from the Eastern states formed the Indian Peace Commission, to find out if the shocking rumors of poverty and poor health on the reservations were true. In 1871, President Grant launched a similar investigation through the Board of Indian Commissioners, which would oversee the Bureau of Indian Affairs. These civilian groups discovered that many of the Indians were near starvation because corrupt agents had stolen the money allocated for buying supplies for the reservation.

Many of the corrupt agents were replaced with leaders of various Christian religious denominations. Some of the worst conditions were changed for the better. Often, however, the religious groups, which divided the tribes between them, were more interested in converting the Indians to Christianity than in alleviating their immediate suffering.

At least one Quaker missionary was remembered as a true leader by an Arapaho artist named Carl Sweezy, who lived on a reservation in Oklahoma: "There was more than one white man's road that we might take, and President Grant wanted us to take the right one. He sent Brinton Darlington to be our first Agent." Darlington brought other Quakers with him who helped plant orchards and gardens, and built good housing, schools, and trading posts. "He was patient and kind; he managed like a chief," says Sweezy.[6]

A young anthropologist named Clark Wissler, who later became Curator of Ethnology at the American Museum of Natural History, traveled around the country west of the Mississippi for several years at the turn of the century. His portraits of Indians and early reservation life, while retaining the superior attitude toward a different race that was typical of white men of his generation, is compassionate and detailed. In a chapter titled "The Great Depression in Indian Country," he presents a report made by an agent at the Blackfeet reservation in Montana in 1884:

> When I entered upon the duties of agent, I found the Indians in a deplorable condition. Their supplies had been limited and many of them were gradually dying of starvation. I visited a large number of their tents and cabins the second day after they had received their weekly rations. . . . All bore marks of suffering from lack of food but the little children seemed to have suffered most; they were so emaciated that it did not seem possible for them to live long; and many of them have since passed away.[7]

This agent was clearly appalled by the situation and by the fact that the reservation simply did not receive enough food for the twenty-three hundred Indians who lived there. He was forced to open and use food that had been condemned, and he reported that Indians were reduced to stripping bark from trees along the creeks and eating the inner portion because they were so hungry. These were people who had hunted the buffalo, by then almost extinct. "This great economic and spiritual depression involved far more tribes than had been caught up in the toils of any other reservation calamity," says Wissler.[8]

The entire economy of the tribes had collapsed. "For confronting the Indian was a forbidding and uninspiring outlook. No longer could he look forward to the long hunting expeditions so dear to him, but what was worse all the worthy aspirations and ambitions sanctioned by his culture were thwarted."[9]

Conditions on the reservations gradually improved in the last years of the nineteenth century. The threat of Indian uprisings had ended. The Indian became, thanks to pulp magazine stories and Buffalo Bill's Wild West show, which staged Indian fights, part of the "romantic West" mythology. What was happening to the real Indian was never part of this mythology. The former "owners" of America were living out their lives on various reservations, and continuing, as best they could, their own customs.

Making a Home

American Indians on the early reservations still lived in tipis, longhouses, hogans, and other Indian homes as often as they could. They also liked to get permission to visit far away reservations. In the Plains, they would load their tipis and equipment on travois (a kind of sled made of poles, which was pulled by horses or dogs), and camp along the way. This enabled them to live in the old way, with each other and without the agent and the store, at least for a short time.

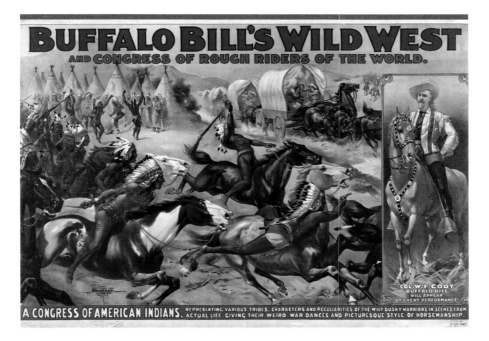

Buffalo Bill's Wild West Show used American Indians for entertainment. It did not convey the hardships they faced.

On each reservation was the agency store. Here Indians gathered to spend whatever money they had been allotted, though some goods were still traded. Since most Indians in the early reservation days could not read or write, they were at the mercy of the trader when they handed over a check for goods. Having been cheated so many times by dishonest traders, the Indian shopper was distrustful of everyone. Since leaving the reservation required a permit, the Indian had little opportunity to spend money in a town. The trader and the high price of goods kept him in debt. The life of the reservation centered around the store, where much-needed blankets, clothing, and food could help against the constant hunger and cold.

The puzzling differences in the perception of property were not the only difficulties facing mere existence on the reservation. The dispensing of medicine was very difficult because the Indians had such completely different ideas about illness and death than those of white people. Traveling doctors, often much respected by their Indian patients, found that the concept of medical prescriptions was difficult to get across. If, after the first dose of medicine, the patient was not feeling much better, he would refuse to take any more. When a medicine to be rubbed on the skin was left with the patient, if it felt good, the rest often was used all at once. Similarly, if cough medicine was given and it did not taste too bad, the whole bottle would be drunk at once. The reasoning was that if it worked, it should all be used.

Wissler made many Indian friends in his travels, and his observations broadened his perspective on their value systems: "It is not difficult to realize . . . that though a white man and an Indian may walk side by side, they do not see alike . . . each may justly regard the other as a fool."[10]

CHAPTER Nine

Indian Land for Sale

The years from 1890 to 1915 still saw occasional rebellions on the outskirts of reservations in the West. These were led by young American Indian men, bored and confused, who had no elders to guide them in the kind of leadership their people needed. Occasionally, during this time, sightings were reported by hikers of lone Indians disappearing into dense underbrush, often in California where whites had practiced "Indian hunts." There were no reservations in California, and the few Indians left pretended to be Latino so they could make a living as seasonal workers.

Indian Territory Becomes Oklahoma

The bulk of Indian people during this era were struggling with the effects of the Dawes Act and

The Last of His Tribe

The very last member of the Yahi Yana tribe was discovered by barking dogs near a corral in Oroville, California, on August 9, 1911. He was put in jail, but was rescued from local ranchers by scholars T. T. Waterman and A. L. Kroeber. Ishi, as the man came to be called, had escaped the massacres of the 1860s and 1870s. Since then he had been hiding in the mountain terrain. Treated kindly, Ishi helped the ethnographers with knowledge of his soon-to-be extinct tribe.

The last surviving member of the Yahi Yana tribe of northern California, photographed in 1914, demonstrates a call that Yahi Yana hunters used to call rabbits.

When Ishi died in 1916, Waterman wrote a tribute to Ishi, saying that he "had an innate regard for the other fellow's existence, and an inborn considerateness . . . to know him was a rare personal privilege, not merely an ethnological privilege. I feel myself that in many ways he was perhaps the most remarkable personality of his century."[1]

living on their reservations. In 1897, President William McKinley announced that Indian Territory would become part of the United States. Through outright stealing and land grabs, what remained of Indian lands was lost. The certainty that even a small parcel of land would be safe from white land grabbing decreased with each new administration.

In 1901, an act was passed which allowed roads to be built through an allotment. If an Indian's land happened to be in the way of the road, the land would be condemned and returned to government use. This action is called *eminent domain* and is still taken against Americans, on occasion, today. "The thrust of government policy remained aimed at negating any sense of cultural wholeness," says Nabokov.[2] Another act in 1907 allowed the government to distribute money that was supposed to be for American Indian nations to individuals, thus once again reducing the idea of shared land and assets.

In Indian Territory, where Cherokee and other "removed" Indians had made a new and prosperous home, much land had already been taken away by the government. Indian Territory then became Oklahoma Territory. (Oklahoma did not become a state until 1907.) When the Dawes Act was passed in 1887, nineteen Indian Territory tribes had voted against it. They now fought for an all-Indian state to be named after Sequoyah, the Cherokee who had invented his people's alphabet. They lost this fight,

Shrinking Allotments

Historian Peter Nabokov uses this example to illustrate the problem of allotments:

> Lizette Denomie was a Chippewa allottee who died in 1897. Her 80 acre plot was split up among nine heirs: twenty years later six of them had died, subdividing the land further so that fourteen of these third-generation heirs had only patches of between four-and-a half acres to three-quarters of an acre apiece. Finally, in 1935, the original tract had been splintered among thirty-five heirs, seventeen of them expected to make a living on less than an acre each.[3]

and yet as late as 1912, two thousand Cherokee, though living in terrible poverty, had still refused to claim their allotments. Even those who did move onto allotments had no security. The problem of inheritance, as heirs tried to divide the small parcels of land between them, meant there was simply not enough land left on which to make a living.

Indian Land Seized

When oil was discovered on the lands of the Osage, Creek, Seminole, and Delaware tribes, land grabbers went to quite incredible lengths to obtain deeds to Indian lands. "False wills were drafted. Indian family members were bribed, beatings and even murder were not uncommon," says Nabokov.[4]

Of the 30 million acres deeded to Indian individuals during allotment, only 3 million were left by

1920. By 1956, members of the Cherokee, Chickasaw, Choctaw, Creek, and Seminole nations owned only 326,902 acres of trust land. This was 1.6 percent of the territory they had been promised they would live on "forever," which had been still intact as of 1898.[5]

It may seem odd that Indians, who had been systematically pursued, killed, cheated, and confined by the government would be willing to go to war for the United States in World War I. Some wanted access to the high status that could come with combat experience. Some belonged to clans, or groups of families, that were protector clans. Some wanted adventure and opportunity. Some felt patriotic toward the United States. Or perhaps it was the chance to be an active part of almost anything, instead of sitting around a reservation getting inadequate handouts. The reasons that drove twenty-five thousand young Indian men to join the United States army and navy varied.

Even more remarkable is that ten thousand Indian Red Cross volunteers, almost all women, sewed one hundred thousand pieces of clothing for overseas troops. They also made sure that five hundred Christmas boxes were sent abroad. Despite their poverty, Indians bought $25 million dollars in war bonds.[6]

Designated for the highest French honor for bravery was Joseph Oklahombi, a Choctaw Indian from Wrighttown, Oklahoma. This extraordinary

American Indians contributed to war efforts during World War II. These American Indian Marine Corps reservists pose for a photo in 1943.

soldier used the same incredible courage, speed, and athletic ability that had threatened U.S. troops during the Indian Wars, to run through seemingly impenetrable barbed wire and open trenches to overpower machine-gun nests as a U.S. soldier during World War II. Oklahombi captured German prisoners, pinpointed strategic enemy strongholds, and rescued wounded soldiers.

While Indians were demonstrating their skills and their loyalty to the war effort, the economic impact of the war harmed the tribes at home. Indian lands were the first to lose funding if the government needed extra money for wartime needs.

However, change was coming. The deplorable conditions at the Indian boarding schools, which included widespread tuberculosis and an eye infection called trachoma, began to be noticed. The Federal Indian Health program and the Society of American Indians founded in 1908 and 1906, respectively, worked hard to bring healthier conditions to these schools. Despite the cruel conditions, some of the graduates retained their pride in their Indian heritage and also learned the skills to make a positive impact in the world. After World War I, the short-lived Society of American Indians and a dedicated white man, John Collier, would begin improvements for American Indians.

CHAPTER Ten

Indian Reorganization

Particularly important to the self-governance that would come out of the debate around the Indian Reorganization Act was a man named John Collier. People who work very hard for a particular cause have often had some setbacks in their lives that changed their philosophy forever. Collier's parents died young. A scandal over business finances left them broken in spirit and contributed to Collier losing faith in the American notion of success. How much land and money a person had was a goal that often backfired. Rather than work toward the kind of assimilation (the joining of cultures so all customs are alike) that the Dawes Act hoped to impose on the Indians, Collier came to believe in what is called multiculturalism. He believed that all the different peoples of the United States should keep their own traditional customs, languages, music, and religion. He believed that human beings needed the experience, the ritual, and spiritual joining of a true community in order to lead fulfilled lives.

Collier's Goals

Collier's early reform efforts were aimed at immigrants in large cities. When he was introduced through a friend to the Pueblo Indians, whose reservation is in New Mexico, he was fascinated. The very communal experience that legislation such as the Dawes Act had tried to kill in the native population was, for Collier, what human beings needed to survive. He did not believe that this communal American Indian spirit was doomed to extinction and he intended to help revive it.

The Pueblo Indians were well-organized farmers and lived quietly, so they were not regulated severely by the U.S. government. Through a complex interweaving of old treaties and new legislation, the Pueblo Indians found themselves about to lose title to some lands and much of their water rights and soon would face massive federal regulation. The Bursum Bill before Congress in 1922 would have destroyed the Pueblo culture.

By this time, John Collier was working with the Pueblo, along with white artists and writers who had settled in New Mexico and appreciated the

A group of Pueblo Indians sent a delegation to the U.S. Capitol in 1923 to appear before a Senate Lands Committee.

Pueblo way of life. Collier organized a protest, sending Pueblo singers and dancers on tour across the country, including large cities such as Chicago and New York, on their way to Washington, D.C. Indians, having had their lands taken, were being looked at very differently in the twentieth century than in the nineteenth. A large public protest in the form of letters and telegrams flooded the White House in support of the Pueblo's position. In March 1923, the Bursum Bill's supporters stopped trying to get it passed.

Government Interference

The Bureau of Indian Affairs (BIA), however, continued to attack the religious and cultural practices of all tribes, particularly the Pueblo and the Hopi. In answer to this attack, Collier formed the American Indian Defense Association (AIDA), which pledged to preserve Indian religion and the dances and other rituals associated with it. He faced great opposition from Christian religious groups who still wanted to "civilize" the Indians. Collier's great determination finally won out and along the way he gathered and publicized information about the BIA's mishandling of rations, health, and education on the reservations.

The director of the Institute for Government Research, Lewis Meriam, conducted an investigation that he published in *The Problem of Indian Administration*. The Meriam report came out in 1928, right before the stock market crash and the beginning of the Great Depression. Meriam's report condemned the Dawes Act and allotment system not only as a total failure, but the cause of the terrible financial burden on the nation from the inefficient and corrupt BIA.

The New Deal

Reacting to the Great Depression, when many people lost their jobs and suffered from extreme poverty, President Franklin Delano Roosevelt initiated reforms that became known as the New Deal. Elected in 1932, Roosevelt appointed John Collier as the commissioner of the Bureau of Indian Affairs, the same agency Collier had been battling for ten years. Collier used the Meriam Report to initiate the 1934 Indian Reorganization Act (IRA), which ended allotment. This would create its own difficulties. Years of getting used to the allotment system and the breakdown of group unity that it was designed to and did bring about on some reservations, could not be overturned with a single stroke.

Collier believed that going back to the idea that everyone in an American Indian group shared use of the land equally was the basis of the kind of community that could save the tribes. However, "The Dawes Act had left many reservations hopelessly checker boarded and fragmented. Often, the best land had been removed from trust status and sold," says historian James Wilson.[1]

Collier managed to get his bill through Congress, but not without great difficulty. Many of the IRA's best provisions were difficult to implement, but would lead to future reforms and tribal self-governance.

Collier quickly managed to bring about an Indian New Deal within the larger New Deal reforms.

Reforms

There were several reforms in the Indian Reorganization Act that were designed to correct some of the damage done to American Indian societies.

1. All further allotment was prohibited.
2. Money was set aside to buy more land for the American Indians.
3. Money was allocated for the tribes to set up business corporations, and they were encouraged to form their own governments.

The need to cut down on government spending helped Collier and other reformers bring more self-sufficiency to reservation government. However, Collier and his reforms were often looked on as too controlling. "Struggles over how tribes should be governed and by whom have been present since the inception of the Indian Reorganization Act," says historian George Russell.[2]

Though Collier is much admired, he remains a controversial figure for many Indian and non-Indian peoples. (For instance, he ordered the destruction of thousands of Navajo sheep. Consequently, the Navajo never adopted the IRA and did not reorganize their government until much later.) Sometimes, in his romantic views of the communal life, he misunderstood "the enormous diversity of [American Indian] culture . . . [and that] as a result of Euro-American

Corruption

Below are some examples of specific Bureau of Indian Affairs corruption:

1. A government agency built a bridge in Arizona on a road never used by Navajo people. The funding came from the Navajo tribal treasury.
2. Paiute water rights in Nevada were diverted to non-Indian water usage.
3. Flathead Indian lands in Montana were turned over to a power company without consulting the Flathead.

contact, most tribes had lost far more of their own traditions than the Pueblos and that some had changed so much" that they really had almost disappeared, according to historian James Wilson.[3]

American Indians Off the Reservations

During the years leading up to the reforms John Collier supported, some Indians left the reservation to make their living in the white world. Indians all around the country were distinguishing themselves, despite discrimination.

In the 1920s, Mohawk Indians of the Caughnawaga tribe, living on a reservation in southern Canada, developed a high-risk, well-paid profession. Indians became the steelworkers who did the precision work on bridges and skyscrapers. They formed a neighborhood in Brooklyn of about two hundred to three hundred Mohawk, and traveled back to the reservation for holidays and on most weekends, driving all night. This group of Indians still participated in the cultural practices of their tribe but had managed to create a specialty that would support them monetarily in the modern world. Mohawk Indians still work together in the steel industry today.[4]

The all-around physical fitness and health of American Indians was far superior to their European conquerors—until diseases and bad housing and poverty took their toll. Athletes such as Jim Thorpe, the famous track star, and winning football teams from the Carlisle and Red Cloud Indian schools tapped into this natural athletic ability.

Jim Thorpe poses in his Carlisle Indian School football uniform.

White reformers and artists, who had left large cities to find new values in nature, often in the Southwest, appreciated the very Indian qualities earlier settlers had tried to destroy. However, this was largely symbolic. Indians were looked on as people from the past, idealized romantically, and the individual Indian, struggling with poverty due to the corruption of the BIA in the reservation system, was mostly ignored. Indians still continued to lose land, lose their children to harsh boarding schools, and be expected to be farmers, even if they lived on desert-like land.

Historian Philip Deloria said:

> Here, then, is one of the paradoxes of Indian country in the twentieth century; if Indians change, their culture is considered contaminated and they lose their 'Indianness'. If they do not change, they remain Indians, but are refused a real existence in the modern world. . . . Defining oneself as an Indian in the twentieth century has meant walking a fine line between the domination and allure of American culture and the resistance and resilience of one's own tradition.[5]

What does it mean to be an Indian in the present? And how does the reservation system either help or hamper present-day Indians?

CHAPTER Eleven

From Protests to the Present

"I like living in this community, and I like being Choctaw; but that's all there is to it. Just because I don't want to be a white man doesn't mean I want to be some mystical Indian either. Just a real human being."

Beasley Denson, Secretary Treasurer of
the Choctaw Tribal Council, 1988[1]

The Indian New Deal and the Indian Reorganization Act (IRA) sought, among other things, to give tribes more economic security on their reservations. While there was some success, the legislation presented large challenges to Indian societies. American Indians were asked to form American-style governments that did not match well with their cultural practices. However, the IRA established Indian societies as dependent domestic nations with a right to govern their own people, which reaffirmed each nation's sovereignty. "It is, after all, a recognition in law of the fact that Indian societies were here first," remarks historian Philip Deloria.[2]

Employment

The Indian New Deal also created opportunities for paid labor on thirty-three reservations. The Indian Emergency Conservation Work (IECW) programs provided training and experience in money and resource management. During the Depression, when large numbers of people around the country were out of work and hungry, the IECW saved the lives of many Indian families. Eighty-five thousand Indians participated in the program and learned skills that would help them in off-reservation work, especially during World War II.[3]

John Collier had employed a great many Indians at the BIA before he resigned as its Commissioner in 1945. By then, both the Senate and the House of Representatives were again complaining that the BIA was spending too much money and had not completed the task of making reservations self-sufficient. Because the tribes had some skill in legal and political matters within their own reservations, they made an attempt to form an organization that would be a political forum for all tribes. The National Council of American Indians

(NCAI) banded together to oppose a policy known as "termination."

Indians had acquired skills through programs put in place by the Indian New Deal and gained experience through the large numbers of Indians who had been involved in World War II. As in World War I, record numbers of American Indians joined the war effort. One third of all able-bodied Indian men joined some branch of the armed services.[4] Many others worked in war industries and volunteer programs. Again, war bonds were purchased by more Indian people per amount of income than any other American group.

The Choctaw telephone code talkers during World War I began the code talking tradition that continued in World War II. One of the most famous instances of Indian involvement in World War II was the Navajo Code Talkers. Though other tribes helped in encoding and deciphering for the army, such as the Oneida, Chippewa, Sauk, Fox, and Comanche, the Marine Corps developed a program that included four hundred Navajo (Dineh) code talkers. They developed and used a special military dictionary using Navajo words for battle directions and machinery.

Unfortunate Assimilation

Unfortunately, the respect for individual Indians who fought in World War II did not extend to respect for

Always a Warrior

American Indian soldiers who served everywhere World War II was fought won many honors. Joseph Medicine Crow, a member of the Crow tribe, recalled his experience:

> When I went to Germany I never thought about war honors, or the four 'coups' which an old-time Crow warrior had to earn in battle. Those days were gone. But afterwards, when I came back and went through this telling of the war deeds ceremony, why, I told my war deeds, and lo and behold I completed the four requirements to become a chief.[5]

Indian culture and life. This was hurtful and frustrating to Indians returning from fighting valiantly in the American cause. John Collier's dream of a multicultural society in which many races, religions, and cultures could live side by side, was overwhelmed by the wish that everyone be the same. And that "same" was mainstream white America. The 1950s was a particularly difficult time for diversity, as the cold war and the fear of different types of government caused suspicion and intolerance against many groups of people. Some Americans even thought that tribalism was similar to Communism.

Assimilation—Indians being absorbed into white society without recognition of their own culture—became the governmental goal. A 1946 Indian Claims Commission, formed to clear up any disputed treaty claims, was coupled with yet another

"Long Promises" Fall Short

Chief Piapot, Cree, spoke in 1895 about reservations:

> In order to become sole masters of our land they relegated us to small reservations as big as my hand and made us long promises as long as my arm; but the next year the promises were shorter and got shorter every year until now they are the length of my finger, and they keep only half of that.[6]

relocation policy. This one, instead of the infamous Trail of Tears leading toward future reservations, was formed to *dissolve* those reservations and send Indians off to cities. This completely contradicted the idea of an Indian cultural revival.

Poverty Still A Problem

Many reservations had again become pockets of poverty during the time that so many energetic young Indian people were involved in World War II. It was confusing to have been in France and Germany with army wages and come home to a reservation that was rural, had no jobs to offer, and held many people, old and young, who felt confused and discouraged. Offered job training by the government, a one-way ticket, a shoddy apartment, and an alarm clock—so they could get up on time to go to work—many native people left the reservation for cities.

When they had to compete for jobs in an urban setting, Indians encountered prejudice and

A woman walks with her daughter toward the makeshift homes at Kickapoo village near Eagle Pass, Texas, in November 1980.

discrimination. They often became just as poor and discouraged as they had been at home on the reservation. Only now, they were isolated culturally as well. There was, for many, a gradual return to the reservation, where at least family could be counted on to help.

Herding wide-ranging, well-organized tribes onto small portions of their land, called reservations, caused terrible misery. Ironically, after World War II, the termination of reservations threatened to bring about what many people thought was inevitable in the nineteenth century, the possible extinction of American Indian culture.

The termination policy was legally passed in 1953. Each state was to deal with this law. When it was completely implemented, Indians would cease to exist as an entity to be dealt with separately by the government. There would be no more governmental responsibility toward American Indians.

Termination was not about freedom, it was about the government no longer being responsible for the tribes they had put on the reservations in the first place. What Indians wanted was to be recognized as Indians with tribal identification as well as American citizenship. The NCAI helped them speak up against termination. By the late 1940s, Indians had fought for America in two world wars. Some had college degrees, and the reforms of the IRA and the Indian New Deal had brought them legal and political skills.

Loss of Prosperity

The Menominee are American Indians in Wisconsin who were running a thriving lumber and sawmill business on their reservation in the 1940s. Though there was no good reason for this successful reservation to be terminated, the government pressured the Menominee to do so. They were offered money to compensate for U.S. Forest Service mismanagement—7.6 million dollars. But, that money would only be given to them if they agreed to terminate the reservation and become a county. Then, all sorts of new government regulations were insisted upon.

The Menominee fought this termination from 1947 to 1961. When the whole tribe had sunk into poverty because of corrupt white control, they struggled to regain their federal trust position. The same thing happened to the Klamath, living on a 1.3 million-acre reservation. They were prosperous on land that was coveted for timber and ranching. Meanwhile, the Klamath fell into chronic poverty.

Congress agreed, in 1958, to only terminate a tribe if the termination was voluntary. By this time, organized, skilled opposition from tribal representatives had begun to have an effect.

Alaska became a state in 1959. The state was offered 103 million acres of federal land that could be developed commercially. This would help the state become economically successful. As in past land-grabs all over the United States, the government did not bother to consult, or even learn about how Alaskan Indians used the lands in question. Because of the highly organized work of the Alaska Federation of Natives (AFN), in 1966 a freeze was placed on land selection—including the Trans-Alaska pipeline construction. By 1971, The Alaska Native Claims Settlement Act (ANCSA) was passed. "Under ANSCA, native people were given $962 million and forty-four million acres of land," says historian Philip Deloria. Eighty thousand Alaska natives with very different interests and work lives had banded together to make this possible. However, even this landmark legislation was controversial because it was based on American political and business structures.[7]

Political Movements

In the rest of the country, the New Frontier, Great Society, and War on Poverty programs helped Indians join the political struggle for employment, legal solutions to problems on the reservations, and better management of funds and resources. But often, political freedom is not without political struggle. The 1960s and early 1970s were a time of rebellion against social and gender inequalities. This became known as "identity politics" and for some American Indians it meant a return to tribal rituals and practices of the past. The National Indian Youth Council (NIYC) of

1961 and the American Indian Movement (AIM), started in the mid-1960s, staged public events to air their grievances against the government.

Two early protests were the sit-in at the deserted prison Alcatraz Island, and the Trail of Broken Treaties march to BIA headquarters. However, the protest most Americans remember occurred at Wounded Knee. Revisiting the scene of the massacre at Wounded Knee, South Dakota, activists from AIM and the Oglala Lakota Sioux, who lived on the Pine Ridge reservation, occupied the town. A battle began between government forces and the Indians.

Much more than being a standoff between the government and Indians, Wounded Knee of 1973 represented a conflict "between Indian people who believed in working 'outside the system' and those who found success working within it," says Phillip Deloria.[8] The major achievement of the AIM movement was a document called *The Twenty Points*, which asked for recognition of old treaty promises.

After the Wounded Knee standoff of 1973, Indian activists were persecuted on many fronts. However, the horror over what had happened at Wounded Knee actually sparked increased federal funds and pro-Indian legislation which lasted until the mid-1980s. But then, large-scale social service underfunding again found tribes so impoverished that they were tempted to sell their remaining land. Religious

A group of American Indians occupy the former prison at Alcatraz Island. They stand under graffiti welcoming Indian occupiers to "United Indian property" on the dock of Alcatraz Island.

freedom was again a government target, and federal programs and legal rights were slashed.

Conditions on reservations varied. The Pine Ridge reservation, according to national statistics on poverty, was declared the poorest county in the United States. Unemployment rates for most reservations were very high. The side effects of poverty and no work are crime, domestic abuse, diabetes, and depression. Alcoholism was a particular problem, and long, straight roads in sparsely populated areas are often lined with white crosses symbolizing Indians who died in auto accidents while intoxicated. The incidence of babies born with fetal alcohol syndrome due to a mother's alcohol consumption increased, as did the threat of AIDS. Suicide rates are high. Indian reservations have the worst health care in the country. For instance, the nearest surgical facility to the Rosebud Sioux reservation is four hours away.

There are, however, stories about successful adaptation. "The BIA," says George Russell, "is not the enemy. In fairness to the BIA today, it should be understood that, in 176 years, many past sins and much of the chaos was institutionalized and inherited. I personally know and have worked with BIA personnel over the years who are capable and dedicated."[9]

What is happening now on reservations? And, what does the future hold?

CHAPTER Twelve

Indian Reservations Now and in the Future

The Bureau of Indian Affairs (BIA) manages almost 56 million acres of reservation land. This land is held in trust by the federal government and reserved for American Indians. Nearly half of the reservation population is non-Indian (46 percent) and 11 million acres of land within reservations is owned by non-Indians (20 percent). This came about largely through long-term effects of the Dawes Allotment Act.[1]

The Navajo Nation

The Navajo Nation encompasses the largest geographical territory of any reservation—17 million acres in four states, with 110 community chapters. The Navajo have a history of adapting in order to survive. No alcohol is allowed on reservation

A Navajo woman and her daughter weave on a loom on their reservation. The Navajo have been able to earn money by selling their crafts to tourists.

territory, and tourist trips through historic land such as Canyon De Chelly must be led by a Navajo guide. Navajo weavers and silversmiths have made a name for themselves worldwide, and the Navajo customs and religious ceremonies are still practiced throughout the beautiful but largely nonagricultural land of the reservation.

Traditional vs. Modern

Reservations do not look like they did in the mid-and late-nineteenth century. With some exceptions, they hold towns with stores and streets of houses, schools, and other public buildings. The most notable exception to this is the Hopi reservation town on top of Hopi mesa in Arizona. There the inhabitants live in pueblo-style houses that take a visitor back to the days before Columbus.

At the Taos Pueblo in New Mexico, the traditional pueblo housing is constantly refurbished and improved, though there is still no electricity or running water. The Navajo reservation still has a few traditional dwellings called hogans.

Many reservations hold ceremonies, some open to the public, that recreate the rituals and dances of the past. The Assiniboine reservation in northeast Montana still has the frames of sweat lodges along the Missouri river. These are used actively by tribal members, whose daily lives are the same as non-Indians in terms of work and school. Most reservations are still well below the national average in poverty and health statistics. The level of organization in the tribal government varies widely from reservation to reservation.

Conservation

Recently, the Cocopah Indians south of Yuma, Arizona, have started a restoration project on the

Colorado River. This is an excellent example of cooperation between private and governmental agencies and the leadership of a small tribe. The Cocopah reservation was established in 1917 and made larger in 1985. It is divided into three separate parts and as little as twenty years ago held five thousand Cocopah Indians. Now the population has sunk to eight hundred. The Colorado River that ran through the reservation began to slowly drain away because of the dam upriver. Many fish species became extinct. This affected not only the Cocopah themselves who fished the river, but an ecotourism fishing industry the Cocopah were hoping would help them financially.

With grants from the BIA, the Environmental Protection Agency, the Bureau of Land Management, and the National Wildlife Federation, restoration projects are under way. These include removal of invasive salt cedar trees that choked out the native plants that allowed a large population of birds to thrive. Negotiations continue to allow more water to be diverted back along the stretch of the Colorado River that is on the reservation. Says tribal elder Colin Soto, "The thing that ties me back to history is the river. If we restore it, we will be able to not only have some rejuvenation of our culture but be able to take people from town and the schools and say, 'This is who I am. This is Cocopah.'"[2]

Today's Definition of a Tribe

What is an American Indian tribe today? The legal definition is "Any Indian tribe, band, nation, rancheria, pueblo, colony or community which is recognized by the United States government as eligible for programs and services provided by the Secretary of the Interior to Indians because of their status as Indians."[3]

Similar conservation projects are under way on the Ute reservation in Colorado and the Walker River Paiute reservation. The devastating effects on water safety of wholesale strip mining on the one remaining official reservation in Oklahoma show up in birth defects and increased cancer rates.[4]

American Indian Casinos

The industry that has gotten the most media attention for the reservations is the gaming industry, the establishment of casinos for legalized gambling. Because reservations are sovereign nations, they do not have to obey the same laws, in most instances, as other states. People who want to gamble can do so without traveling to one of the few legalized gambling spots in the United States. The reservations are also exempt from taxes, so the casinos can generate a great deal of tax-free income for a tribe. The largest casino has been built by the Mashantucket Pequot of Connecticut, a very small remnant of the powerful Pequot confederacy nearly exterminated in the seventeenth century by settlers.

Only 13 percent of Indian nations have gaming and only five or six reservations are generating wealth. However, for those tribes, the prosperity that should be all positive has drawbacks. The sudden presence of the casino and tourists and wealth in formerly poor communities has been disruptive. How do you retain cultural values in the face of the total materialism represented by casino gambling,

Mary Ann Andreas, Morongo Band of Mission Indians Tribal Chairman, stands in front of a bank of slot machines in the Casino Morongo outside Cabazon, California, in March 1998.

originally a non-Indian development? On the Mohawk reservation, the conflict between different factions, the gulf between rich and poor, actually led to armed conflict among tribal members.

This conflict between the new prosperity and traditional values worries some who believe casino gambling may not be good for the tribe in the long run. Historian James Wilson points out:

> Native Americans, they know, are trapped in a perennial Catch-22: if they appear to live up to their stereotype as "poor," "lazy" and "dependent on welfare" they are seen as a drain on the hard-working American taxpayer and provoke calls for the government to stop featherbedding [taking full care of] them; if, on the other hand, they show some initiative and visibly prosper—as the experience of the Five Civilized Tribes [the Cherokee, Chickasaw, Choctaw, Creek, and Seminole nations] and the terminated peoples like the Menominee testify— outraged citizens promptly demand that their reservations should be dissolved and they should be "treated just like anyone else."[5]

American Indian Identity

The Passamaquoddy of Maine won a substantial court victory in 1980, which confirmed their recognition as a tribe and entitled them to federal services and land and good schools. However, these good schools rarely spend much time teaching the native language and often alienate students from their parents. Says Wayne Newell, a tribal member who works in a large Passamaquoddy school, "To witness the dying of your language on a daily basis is a really painful experience . . . It's really painful. And I don't think it's possible for people to really understand unless they're in this predicament."[6]

This leads into what is the largest issue facing Native Americans today: "Who and what is an Indian?"[7]

Because of the dislocations, the uprooting of Indian societies, and the intermarriage with people of other American Indian groups and whites, being an Indian is not just a tribal affiliation. Saginaw-Chippewa historian George Russell speaks of this as racially hyphenated Indians. Who is Indian, "either by legal definition or by self-identification, has become an important issue for Indians and their respective tribes."[8]

Self-identified Indians number 2,476,000. This comes from the Census 2000 form that says that if you mark a certain box you are counted as an Indian. However, 22 percent of those Indians (538,000) live on the reservation, and 78 percent (1,938,000) live elsewhere. Only 1.7 million off-reservation Indians are enrolled tribal members. In addition, it is estimated that some 15 million people "believe they have an Indian ancestor but have lost their tribal connection," says George Russell.[9]

These figures reveal three critical problems facing today's Indian population. One of these is blood quantum. This means not only how much Indian versus non-Indian blood a person might have, but how much of which tribal blood an Indian has. For instance, even if an Indian were full-blood, points out historian George Russell, "if a Navajo man marries a Hopi woman; and their Navajo-Hopi son marries a Sioux-Crow wife; and their Navajo-Hopi-Sioux Crow grandson marries a Pima-Kaw-Apache-Ute wife; their great-grandchildren are Navajo-Hopi-Sioux-Crow-Pima-Kaw-Apache-Ute."[10]

In just four generations, these grandchildren, though full-blooded Indians, have one-eighth blood quantum from eight different tribes. Most tribes have a one-quarter blood quantum minimum for membership. Therefore, these grandchildren cannot be members of any of their tribes. Without an enrolled tribal membership, Indians are not eligible for federal programs. Says Russell, "The bottom line is that theoretically, the Indian gene pool will become smaller with each generation until it is extinguished."[11]

Another problem raised by these census statistics is how to continue connections between off-reservation, or urban, American Indians and Indians on the reservation. The loss of tribal language is an obvious outgrowth of these issues. Of the 500 distinct Indian languages spoken in 1492, 350 have already become extinct and 150 are endangered. Predictions from linguists are that by 2050, only twenty Indian languages will remain.[12]

Don Havatone, of the Hualapai, watches the rollout of the Skywalk on the Hualapai Indian Reservation at Grand Canyon West, Arizona, in March 2007. The Hualapai opened it to the public charging twenty-five dollars per person in addition to other entry fees.

A cultural renaissance is taking place within Indian communities and as a result art and environmentalism are flowering. This has led to interest by non-Indians who appreciate Indian art and the ways Indians interacted with the environment.

However, this has not changed the difficulties facing Indian people today. Many economic initiatives

By the Numbers

In the United States, there are 563 federally recognized American Indian governments. Alaska has 228 of those tribes. As of the 2000 census, the size of tribes ranged from several in California with only two or three members to the Navajo Nation with 298,215 members and the Cherokee Nation with 281,000 members. About two hundred tribes are extinct. More than 46 tribes are state-recognized, and 245 tribes are petitioning for federal recognition.[13]

are being formed, with current support from federal and private conservation groups helping them succeed. And yet, the constantly shifting land areas and population groups on reservations, the rate of intermarriage and the still alarming health, education, and employment statistics, pose problems for the future. George Russell places hope for future generations in the hands of his own people:

> American Indian destiny is at a crossroads. Indians must prepare to take control of their destiny, as gently as possible. The next battles will be won by attorneys whose weapons are the legal briefs and laptop computers . . . American Indians have the responsibility, to those ancestors who fired arrows against cannons and survived against overwhelming odds, to make that survival meaningful.[14]

Timeline

1492	Columbus arrives in the New World and thinks he has reached the East Indies. He calls the native population "Indians."
1539	Hernando de Soto reaches the Southeast. He systematically slaughters the inhabitants and spreads disease.
1607	Jamestown colony is founded by a group of English settlers.
1620	Plymouth colony is founded by a group of English colonists; many of them seek freedom to worship as they choose.
1744	Treaty of Lancaster is signed.
1775	American Revolution begins with most Indian tribes on the British side.
1776	Declaration of Independence is signed and distributed.
1778	First treaty between Indians and the new United States government.
1783	American Revolution is over, with negative results for Indian independence.
1803	Louisiana Purchase opens up the West; Lewis and Clark prepare to explore.

1824	Bureau of Indian Affairs (BIA) is established.
1830	Indian Removal Act is passed. This leads to thousands of families being marched to Indian Territory. Many die along the "Trail of Tears."
1848	Gold is discovered in California and miners and settlers pour into American Indian lands.
1850	United States legislation stops all foreign land claims.
1854	Indian Appropriation Act legalizes the reservations that the territories had established for Indians during the implementation of the Removal Act of 1830.
1861–1865	Civil War is fought. Many tribes are forced to take sides, and funds for reservations are even scarcer.
1864	The Navajo Long Walk begins.
1868	Fort Laramie peace conference is held. Ten Sioux tribes and the Arapahoe sign treaties.
1870	Ghost Dance religion begins, drawing many tribes into a hope for spiritual renewal.
1871	End of treaties between United States and Indians.

1876	Defeat of General Custer at the Little Big Horn in Montana by Sioux and Cheyenne warriors.
1879	Carlisle Indian School, in Pennsylvania, is founded.
1887	Dawes Allotment Act subdivides American Indian lands into single-family acreage.
1890	The Battle of Wounded Knee occurs. American troops massacre more than three hundred Sioux and Cheyenne men, women, and children.
1895	Only a thousand buffalo are left on the plains; American Indians are forced to move to reservations to avoid starvation.
1917–1919	United States enters World War I; American Indian soldiers distinguish themselves in battle.
1924	American Indians become United States citizens.
1934	Indian Reorganization Act ends allotment but severe checkerboarding of reservation land creates confusion and more poverty.
1941–1945	United States enters World War II; Navajo code talkers are used extensively.
1944	National Congress of American Indians is created.

1946	Indian Claims Commission Act, originally established to help Indians settle claims against the U.S. government, leads to BIA efforts at relocation.
1954	Termination and Relocation Act sends seventeen thousand Indians from the reservations to the cities.
1973	Returning from a march on Washington, D.C., to protest "Trail of Broken Treaties," Indians take over the town of Wounded Knee.
1975	Indian Self-Determination and Education Assistance Act.
1978	American Indian Religious Freedom Act and the Indian Child Welfare Act.
1988	Indian Gaming Regulatory Act allows several tribes to start gambling casinos on their reservations.
1989	Smithsonian Institution consolidates Indian collections.
1994	The Smithsonian's National Museum of the American Indian (NMAI) facility opens in New York City.
1999	Another NMAI facility opens in Suitland, Maryland.
2004	NMAI's main facility and museum opens on the National Mall in Washington, D.C.

CHAPTER *Notes*

CHAPTER 1. Battling for Freedom

1 | Peter Nabokov, in Betty Ballantine and Ian Ballantine, eds., *The Native Americans: An Illustrated History* (North Dighton, Mass.: World Publications Group, 2001), p. 346.

2 | John Keegan, *Fields of Battle: The Wars for North America* (New York: Albert A. Knopf, 1996), p. 287.

CHAPTER 2. Before the Reservations

1 | Charles C. Mann, *1491, New Revelations of the Americas Before Columbus* (New York: Alfred A. Knopf, 2005), p. 94.

2 | George Russell, *American Indian Facts of Life* (Phoenix, Ariz.: Russell Publications, 2004), p. 25.

3 | Mann, p. 105.

4 | Russell, p. 39.

5 | Mann, p. 105.

6 | Ibid., p. 185.

7 | Ibid., p. 192.

8 | Ralph K. Andrist, in Clark Wissler, *Red Man Reservations* (New York: Collier Books, 1971), p. ix.

9 | Russell Thornton, *American Indian Holocaust and Survival: A Population History Since 1492* (Norman, Okla.: University of Oklahoma Press, 1987), p. 35.

10 | Richard White, in Betty Ballantine and Ian Ballantine, eds., *The Native Americans: An Illustrated History* (North Dighton, Mass.: World Publications, 2001), p. 265.

CHAPTER 3. The Decline of Independence

1 | George Russell, *American Indian Facts of Life* (Phoenix, Ariz.: Native Data Network, 2004), p. 26.

2 | Richard White, in Betty Ballantine and Ian Ballantine, eds., *The Native Americans: An Illustrated History* (North Dighton, Mass.: World Publications Group, 2001), p. 283.

3 | Landon Y. Jones, *William Clark and the Shaping of the West* (New York: Hill and Wang, 2004), p. 21.

4 | Alan Taylor, *The Divided Ground* (New York: Alfred A. Knopf, 2006), p. 32.

5 | James Wilson, *The Earth Shall Weep* (New York: Grove Press, 1998), p. 127.

6 | Jones, p. 22.

7 | Ibid., p. 21.

8 | Ibid., p. 85.

9 | White, p. 293.

CHAPTER 4. Indian Removal

1 | Klaus Frantz, *Indian Reservations in the United States* (Chicago: University of Chicago Press, 1999), p. 13.

2 | Landon Y. Jones, *William Clark and the Shaping of the West* (New York: Hill and Wang, 2004), pp. 279–280.

3 | George Russell, *American Indian Facts of Life* (Phoenix, Ariz.: Native Data Network, 2004), p. 51.

4 | Ibid.

5 | Ibid.

6 | Ibid., p. 77.

7 | Peter Nabokov, in Betty Ballantine and Ian Ballantine, eds., *The Native Americans: An Illustrated History* (North Dighton, Mass.: World Publications Group, 2001), p. 294.

8 | Jones, p. 292.

9 | Ibid., p. 293.

10 | Nabokov, p. 309.

CHAPTER 5. Setting the Stage for Reservations

1 | Peter Nabokov, in Betty Ballantine and Ian Ballantine, eds., *The Native Americans: An Illustrated History* (North Dighton, Mass.: World Publications Group, 2001), p. 312.

2 | Ibid., p. 312.

3 | Landon Y. Jones, *William Clark and the Shaping of the West* (New York: Hill and Wang, 2004), p. 331.

4 | Ibid.

5 | Ibid.

6 | Nabokov, p. 321.

7 | David B. Guralink, ed., *Webster's New World Dictionary* (New York: Simon and Schuster, 1980), p. 1208.

8 | Catherine Soames, ed., *The Oxford Compact English Dictionary* (Oxford, England: Oxford University Press, 2003), p. 968.

9 | James Wilson, *The Earth Shall Weep* (New York: Grove Press, 1998), p. 267.

10 | Ibid., p. 265.

11 | Ibid., p. 270.

12 | Ibid., p. 271.

CHAPTER 6. How the West Was Won

1 | James Wilson, *The Earth Shall Weep* (New York: Grove Press, 1998), p. 240.

2 | William Brandon, *The American Heritage Book of Indians* (New York: Dell Publishing Company, 1971), p. 352.

3 | Wilson, p. 269.

4 | The Council on Interracial Books for Children, ed., *Chronicles of American Indian Protest* (New York: Fawcett Books,1971), p. 235.

5 | Wilson, p. 153.

6 | Peter Nabokov, in Betty Ballantine and Ian Ballantine, eds., *The Native Americans: An Illustrated History* (North Dighton, Mass.: World Publications Group, 2001), p. 316.

7 | Wilson, pp. 280–281.

8 | Nabokov, p. 330.

9 | Ibid.

10 | Ibid.

11 | Ibid., p. 339.

12 | George Russell, *American Indian Facts of Life* (Phoenix, Ariz.: Native Data Network, 2004), p. 34.

CHAPTER 7. Violence and Betrayal

1 | Peter Nabokov, in Betty Ballantine and Ian Ballantine, eds., *The Native Americans: An Illustrated History* (North Dighton, Mass.: World Publications Group, 2001), p. 365.

2 | Ibid., p. 364.

3 | James Wilson, *The Earth Shall Weep* (New York: Grove Press, 1998), p. 285.

4 | Dee Brown, *Bury My Heart at Wounded Knee* (New York: Holt, Rinehart & Winston, New York, 1970), p. 444.

5   Nabokov, p. 366.

6   Ralph K. Andrist, introduction, in Clark Wissler, *Red Man Reservations* (New York: Collier Books, 1972), xiv.

7   George Russell, *American Indian Facts of Life* (Phoenix, Ariz.: Native Data Network, 2004), p. 87.

8   Wilson, p. 305.

9   Nabokov, p. 369.

10   Ibid.

11   Wilson, p. 309.

CHAPTER 8. Indian Schools and Early Life on Reservations

1   James Wilson, *The Earth Shall Weep* (New York: Grove Press, 1998), p. 312.

2   Ibid., p. 315.

3   George Russell, *American Indian Facts of Life* (Phoenix, Ariz.: Native Data Network, 2004).

4   Peter Nabokov, in Betty Ballantine and Ian Ballantine, eds., *The Native Americans: An Illustrated History* (North Dighton, Mass.: World Publications Group, 2001), p. 368.

5   Ibid., p. 341.

6   Ibid., p. 343.

7   Clark Wissler, *Red Man Reservations* (New York: Collier Books, 1971), p. 64.

8   Ibid.

9   Ibid., p. 65.

10   Ibid.

CHAPTER 9. Indian Land for Sale

1   James Wilson, *The Earth Shall Weep* (New York: Grove Press, 1998), p. 245.

2   Peter Nabokov, in Betty Ballantine and Ian Ballantine, eds., *The Native Americans: An Illustrated History* (North Dighton, Mass.: World Publications Group, 2001), p. 373.

3   Ibid., p. 374.

4   Ibid.

5   Ibid., p. 369.

6   Ibid., p. 379.

Chapter 10. Indian Reorganization

1. James Wilson, *The Earth Shall Weep* (New York: Grove Press, 1998), p. 348.

2. George Russell, *American Indian Facts of Life* (Phoenix, Ariz.: Native Data Network, 2004), p. 73.

3. Wilson, p. 357.

4. Philip J. Deloria, in Betty Ballantine and Ian Ballantine, eds., *The Native Americans: An Illustrated History* (North Dighton, Mass.: World Publications, 2001), p. 388.

5. Ibid., p. 403.

Chapter 11. From Protests to the Present

1. Philip J. Deloria, in Betty Ballantine and Ian Ballantine, eds., *The Native Americans: An Illustrated History* (North Dighton, Mass.: World Publications Group, 2001), p. 460.

2. Ibid., p. 416.

3. Ibid.

4. Ibid., p. 422.

5. Ibid., p. 423.

6. Peter Nabokov, in Betty Ballantine and Ian Ballantine, eds., *The Native Americans: An Illustrated History* (North Dighton, Mass.: World Publications Group, 2001), p. 301.

7. Deloria, p. 433.

8. Ibid., p. 441.

9. George Russell, *American Indian Facts of Life* (Phoenix, Ariz.: Native Data Network, 2004), p. 89.

Chapter 12. Indian Reservations Now and in the Future

1. George Russell, *American Indian Facts of Life* (Phoenix, Ariz.: Native Data Network, 2004), p. 89.

2. Jim Morrison, "Emergency Aid For An Ailing River," *National Wildlife Federation Magazine*, Vol. 44, No. 3, (2006), pp. 13–14.

3. Russell, pp. 55–56.

4. Winona La Duke, "Indigenous Environmental Perspectives," *A North American Primer,* in *Akwekon Journal*, Vol. 9, No. 2, (1992), p. 61.

Chapter Notes

5 | James Wilson, *The Earth Shall Weep* (New York: Grove Press, 1998), pp. 417–418.

6 | Ibid., p. 421.

7 | Ibid., p. 422.

8 | Russell, p. 52.

9 | Ibid., p. 56.

10 | Ibid., p. 61.

11 | Ibid., p. 62.

12 | Ibid., p. 65.

13 | Ibid., p. 69.

14 | Ibid., pp. 115 and 143.

Glossary

alliance—A close association for similar goals, often of nations or political parties.

allotment—A share or portion. Indian reservations were subdivided into portions with a certain number of acres, one portion per family.

ecology—The branch of biology that deals with the relations between all living creatures and their environment.

epidemic—The rapid spreading of a contagious disease.

massacre—The killing of large numbers of people.

pandemic—An epidemic that spreads over a large area.

paradox—A statement of condition that seems to be just the opposite of what it says or does but which may in fact be true.

perception—An understanding by the mind or the senses of an idea or a quality.

retaliate—To react to an injury or wrong in the same way it was given.

revitalization—Bringing back energy or spirit after a decline.

spiritual—Having to do with the mind and not the body or material things. For American Indians, it was a tribal and personal connection with nature and land and animals, and of life all around them.

tipi—A cone-shaped tent of animal skins used by the Plains Indians.

trance—A state of changed consciousness, somewhat like sleep. American Indians use trances to reach and express spiritual connection.

treaty—A document representing a formal agreement or contract between two or more nations. Usually this refers to trade, peace, or alliance.

Further Reading

Books

Dunn, John M. *The Relocation of the Native American Indian*. San Diego, Calif.: Lucent Books, 2005.

Isaacs, Sally Senzell. *The Trail of Tears*. Chicago: Heinemann Library, 2004.

Kallen, Stuart A., ed. *Indian Gaming*. San Diego, Calif.: Greenhaven Press, 2006.

McIntosh, Marsha. *Teen Life on Reservations and First Nation Communities: Growing Up Native*. Philadelphia: Mason Crest Publishers, 2007.

Ray, Kurt. *Native Americans and the New American Government: Treaties and Promises*. New York: Rosen Publishing Group, 2004.

Stefoff, Rebecca. *The Indian Wars*. Tarrytown, N.Y.: Benchmark Books, 2003.

Wagner, Katherine. *Life on an Indian Reservation*. Farmington Hills, Mich.: Lecent Books, 2005.

Internet Addresses

The National Museum of the American Indian
<http://www.americanindian.si.edu/>

Native Networks
<http://www.nativenetworks.si.edu/>

The Smithsonian Institution Research Information System (SIRIS)
<http://www.siris.si.edu/>

Index